# Automatic Semantic Interpretation

Jan van Bakel

# Automatic Semantic Interpretation

## A Computer Model of Understanding Natural Language

1984
FORIS PUBLICATIONS
Dordrecht - Holland/Cinnaminson - U.S.A.

*Published by:*
Foris Publications Holland
P.O. Box 509
3300 AM Dordrecht, The Netherlands

*Sole distributor for the U.S.A. and Canada:*
Foris Publications U.S.A.
P.O. Box C-50
Cinnaminson N.J. 08077
U.S.A.

ISBN 90 6765 039 0



Printed in the Netherlands by ICG Printing, Dordrecht.

To Natascha

*Jeugde is minnelijk, elde is treurziek,*
*jeugde is blakende, elde is bloedloos;*
*gij verwekt in mij 't geheugen*
*van de dagen toen ik jong was ...*

Guido Gezelle

# Preface

This study describes a system of syntactic analysis and semantic interpretation of Dutch sentences. It deals with a certain amount of computational linguistic research that was executed at the departement of Computational Linguistics at the Catholic University of Nijmegen, Netherlands.

The start of the project took place as early as 1974, when the first version of AMAZON was built, as a matter of fact a long time before the department of Computational Linguistics was founded. After that time the work on AMAZON was carried on for several years. It successively led to a new version, AMAZON(80), characterized by a morphology separated from the syntax, and to AMAZON(83). While in earlier forms the grammar had been embedded in a SNOBOL computer program, we succeeded at that time in rebuilding it into a contextfree affix grammar. Now we consider AMAZON(83) as the definite first stage of our semantic interpreter.

Only a short time after the first work on AMAZON was finished, we started building the powerful program CASUS that has to do the semantic interpretation strictly speaking, and we designed the semantic language SELANCA (SEmantic LANguage CAsus). CASUS translates AMAZON structures into SELANCA expressions. This translation is of a kind that needs transformational changes: subtrees are deleted, added and moved in order to obtain the expressions intended.

After a general Introduction, section 2 deals with the contextfree affix grammar AMAZON and it's features. Attention is paid to the structures that are assigned to Dutch sentences as well as to the reasons why these structures were chosen. We will also speak about the way the affix grammar is transformed into a normal contextfree grammar. In addition, attention is paid to the form of the lexicon and the morphological routines used.

Chapter 3 deals with CASUS. The first section comments on the semantic language SELANCA as we designed it. Section 3.2 pays attention to the translation process AMAZON-SELANCA. It deals with linguistic theory and details of the way this was implemented. After the concluding chapter and the notes and references, there is an appendix with some technical documentation about the components that constitute the semantic interpreter.

While finishing this book, I feel deep gratitude for, above all, the students in the department of Computational Linguistics in the Litterary Faculty of the Catholic University of Nijmegen. During the last five years a number of alert and critical young people took an important part in the discussions about things that will be dealt with in this study. More of them, too, joined in building program modules to account for pieces of linguistic theory both in the surface syntax AMAZON and in the semantic interpreter CASUS. Without their cooperation and inspiration not much of the project would have been completed, while, at present, quite a lot of this work may be mentioned with some enthusiasm. I would like to thank them all for their participation in one way or another. Some of their names will return in the references, others have been mentioned earlier in some previous articles. With some special emphasis I would like to thank Peter Arno Coppen, who played such a special role in the publication of this study.

Some remarks should be made about the institutional environment, where the research reported took place, viz. the department of Computational Linguistics in the literary faculty of the University of Nijmegen. We are proud of being the first department of Computational Linguistics in a literary faculty in Dutch universities. For a long time we have been the only one, but recently Tilburg too has started with work in the same field. I think we should praise the Faculty's board, that created the possibility to do the education and research activities on the field of computational linguistics, both of which, in a nice interaction, made possible, among other things, what is reported in this book.

Nijmegen, 5 June 1984

# Contents

# 1 Introduction

## 1.1 COMPUTER MODELS OF NATURAL LANGUAGE

The analyzing system AMAZON – CASUS is claimed to be a model of a native speaker's competence of understanding natural language sentences. Computational linguistics, just as linguistics in general, need necessarily claim something like this. The only basis for judging the adequacy of analyses of sentences is a native speaker's intuition. If a formal model of language should not reflect a human faculty, there would be no basis whatsoever to evaluate it. Every evaluation of what is done with or said about linguistic phenomena ultimately depends upon an approval or disapproval that originates in knowledge of natural language. In this sense linguistics necessarily is to be positioned in a mentalistic environment and a merely instrumentalistic orientation seems to be plainly impossible. This is a way of stating that the work reported in this study is not to be considered as an instrumentalistic project. It is linguistic with respect to both it's motivation and it's goal. What is also meant, however, is that a project like ours should not necessarily be viewed as having the intention to pay a contribution to nowadays theoretical linguistics if it claims to be an account of human intuitions about natural language.

A thorough analysis should be made of the relations between theoretical linguistics as it is looked upon nowadays and computational linguistics. With this remark I am aiming at linguistics as it is conceived of in the Chomskyan environment and not to other research programs that also might be considered to be of theoretical linguistic nature. It seems necessary that all linguistic research should legitimize itself in relation with that enterprise. This is especially true for computational linguistics, since it has been a major point of discussion what the position of computer science should be as opposed to theoretical linguistics and it's aims and claims. Therefore, the question has to be answered as to what is the relevance of computational linguistics for theoretical linguistics or, the other way round, of theoretical linguistics for computational linguistics.

For quite a long time the suggestion was made that theoretical linguistics was aiming at a total and final formal characterization of a natural language. The development of theoretical insights from Chomsky's *Syntactic Structures* of 1957 to his core grammar of Chomsky [1979] leads from actualized grammars of specific languages to a universal theory about the structure of human language, without any need to spell out the theory into complete grammars for particular languages. At present, I think, it has to be established, as is done by Koster [1983] in clear words, that e.g. the possibility to generate a natural language with a contextfree grammar, is of complete theoretical irrelevance. Koster does not neglect that, in earlier days, also the work of Chomsky has not always been completely plain in this respect, although he sees passages in *Aspects of a Theory of Syntax* [1965] where Chomsky already shows the later view. The work of Joyce Friedman [1971] certainly has to be considered as an important attempt to make practical use of transformational grammar theory, but it is also based on the conviction that building grammars is the ratio of theoretical linguistics: at one hand the author speakes of *a computational aid to the linguist* but at the other hand she states that *formalization is also of linguistic importance, as Chomsky has often stressed. For example, questions of relative simplicity of grammars are answerable only when some precise notational schema makes the grammars comparable. Even more important, a grammar cannot be said to define a language unless the process of sentence generation is fully specified, so that the sentences are generated in a well-defined way, without appeal to intuition.* At the end of her book she speaks explicitly about *a useful tool for linguistic research*, indicating that building complete grammars is the ratio of theoretical linguistics. These quotations characterize the view on the relations between different disciplines shortly after *Aspects*. Although some allusions are already made in the direction of computational linguistics as a support of theoretical linguistics, there is clearly to be heard the conviction that linguistics is aiming at, or at least should aim at, building grammars for natural languages. At ours Evers and Huybregts [1977] formulated a rather complete grammar of Dutch and German and Kraak and Klooster [1968] remarked that the grammarian should think of a computer as an ideal reader of his grammar, who spells out all the sentences that are defined in it and nothing else, suggesting also that the main task of linguistics is to build complete grammars. Since this idea has been abandoned, computational linguists can no longer claim to be the ultimate sense of theoretical linguistics. Their work has been orphaned so to speak. In 1984, it is no longer possible to claim that building grammars to generate or analyze natural language sentences is the fulfilling of the highest aims of linguistics, or even of any goal of it.

Sometimes computational linguists radically try to save the sense of their work by claiming it's necessary testing function with respect to a developed linguistic theory. Being no longer itself the goal of theoretical linguistics, it declares theoretical linguistics as it's own goal. Formal theories should only be valued, if a computer simulation had shown their correctness. The undecidibility of an example grammar for instance should be considered an essential defect, since it could not garantee to generate or analyze a certain sentence within a finite amount of time. Falsifying the correctness of a proposed transformational rule should be considered a significant contribution to the development of an adequate theory, so theoreticians should realize that computational linguistics had to be considered as the high judge with the decisive judgement. Something like this may be read in e.g. Marcus [1981] where it is argued that some of Chomsky's constraints on transformations *fall out* of the developed grammar interpreter. When Marcus remarks that a certain feature of his interpreter is matching exactly Chomsky's Specified Subject Constraint, he seems to suggest that his computer model functions as an empiric test of that theoretical construct, which should entail, as I am inclined to understand, that computer simulations are suitable means to support linguistic theories. In very much the same way Kempen and Hoenkamp [1982] argue, that their procedural grammar is supporting the locality principle of Koster [1978], also with the suggestion that this support should be of theoretical relevance. I think, however, that computational linguistics is mistaken. It is an obvious fact that theoretical linguistics in it's present orientation is not at all interested in building concrete grammars but only in an explanatory theory about human language, in order to explain that young children can learn their mothertongue in an extremely short time. The idea of a core grammar needs no support at all in the form of an empirical test by computer simulation nor, for that matter, is it aiming at any application on computers. For computational linguistics this seems to be a rather disappointing situation, since it means no less than a total isolation. No linguistic theoretician will change his theories because of whichever computer results. This means, that computational linguistics will have to look for another legitimation, which I think is not difficult.

There is a possible and well to motivate legitimation for building computermodels of linguistic theories. The basic idea of the present study is that, whatever may be said about the main goals of theoretical linguistics, it is legitimate to look at linguistics as an *application oriented research program*. It follows from my remarks above that, in doing so, one does not necessarily leave the mentalistic intentions. What does it mean, however, to say that some research is application oriented? It needs no clarification that application of a certain thing should take place outside the thing in question, and that the object applied should serve as an instrument or as a basis for some activity. Applying a theory has always to do with engineering. Computational linguistics, thus, is theoretical linguistic research that is aimed at application of theoretical linguistic insights in linguistic engineering environments[1].

There are, of course, a number of linguistic applications that can be imagined and it is hardly needed to give examples. Human interaction whith a plane ticket selling robot is an almost classical item. A spoken command or question has to be recognized, analysed and translated into an adequate machine reaction. If the machine is not only expected to listen but also to talk, it will be necessary to build a sentence generator too. Another application would be an automatic message reader on e.g. a railway station, where the information, available in the traffic controling system, would be translated into messages like 'The train from Utrecht with destination Maastricht, which has a delay of 7 minutes and a half, will arrive at platform 12 in 1 minute; passengers are kindly requested to get in quickly'. In this situation the machine only has to be able to transform non linguistic information that is represented in some railway information system into natural language sentences. The problem of building such a machine would only be partly of linguistic nature. A possible application is also a reading machine, to be used by blind people. It is not immediately clear how much linguistic sophistication would be needed in connection with this. A big class of applications, further, is defined as question answering systems, characterized by the presence of a database and a natural language interface which enables asking questions about the database's contents and changing the information by entering natural language commands. Linguistic support of all these systems will have to take into account quite a number of non linguistic matters. But almost all of them would require analyzing and understanding natural language sentences. Considering all this will easily convince people of the relevance of computational linguistic research for future applications. (Automatic translation, at last, should not be lost out of sight.)

Computational linguistics would be of little importance if application of it's theories were a trivial matter, which it is not. Since linguistics in none of it's shapes after 1954 has ever been able to present a theory that could do without deletion, it seems inevitable to end up in a transformational model. It is a well-known fact that a transformational grammar is quite difficult to work with on a computer or, for that matter, by heart. Although generating and analyzing sentences seem to be the inverse of each other, it is not in general possible to invert an analyzing grammar into a generating one or the other way round. As a next point, there is the decidability problem, i.e. the question whether it is possible to decide within a restricted amount of time that a certain sentence is or is not defined by the grammar. Natural languages do not seem to be decidable in general, or at least it seems to be an undecided question whether they are. Computational just as theoretical linguistics will have to constrain the grammar to work with. Since a natural language is richer than contextfree[2], the restriction will regard exclusion of certain types of transformations or, possibly, the definition of a correct context sensitive grammar.

The model we built is an analyzing one. There is a lot to say about analyzing and generating grammars and the sense of working with them[3]. Since for generating, one has to define a mechanism to select the sentences to be generated, the choice for analyzing instead of generating could not be difficult. If one should object to a system that generates the sentences of a certain grammar in the order in which they are defined in it, one has to choose one that works in interaction with some reality. I assume for a moment, that a sentence generator that works by chance would not be acceptable at all. It may be concluded, that automatic sentence generation requires the definition of a piece of the world about which the sentences to be generated should speak[4]. Many scholars build a situation that contains a database or some other model of reality, in connection with which commands and questions in natural language are used. The selecting of the sentences to be generated in these circumstances is constrained by the (model of) the chosen reality. Question answering systems can only be thought of as containing some database, connected with a linguistic module that is able to analyze the natural language sentences of the user, to evaluate them, especially with respect to their meaning relation with the data, and to formulate the result in a natural language sentence which is returned to the user[5]. Thus, even if the system should be built with linguistic intentions, the kind of theoretical issues that may ask for attention is strictly limited and, moreover, the user has to do a lot of things in which he may not be interested at all: if he should be interested mainly in automatic sentence generation, he still has to build a sentence analyzer, and if he wants to concentrate on analyzing sentences, he has to build a sentence generator nevertheless. In all cases, he has to go into questions about organizing databases, even if this might seem to him not to be a very inspiring subject. The reason why I chose for sentence analysis is only that I did not like to be constrained to that little subset of Dutch that would be usable in connection with some database, that I did not like to build a database anyhow before being able to do what somebody who claims to be a linguist should do: to deal with problems of natural language, and that I felt little motivation to build a sentence generator, especially one that should speak of that little part of the world that I could simulate on a machine. An important reason for my personal preference for analyzing certainly is also, that, as Schank [1972, 555] states, in accordance with a similar utterance of Wilks [1977, 354], Chomsky's syntax based transformational-generative grammar cannot seriously be proposed as a theory of human understanding (nor is intended as such). To find sentences to analyze or, to speak more generally, syntactic problems and crucial sentences to represent them, cannot be a problem. Building a model that embodies an interesting subset of Dutch with a possibility to concentrate on special syntactic subjects, is the best one can do. Our syntax AMAZON is a nice instrument. It has no rigidity at all as far as it's lexicon is concerned. It accepts an interesting subset of Dutch, assigning to the sentences interesting structures which are rich in syntactic information. The semantic analyzer CASUS, the part of the model that plays the most important role in this report, is likewise nicely flexible, since it is only the external lexicon which should be adapted for new sentences. The present report will try to carry over these ideas to the reader.

After Marcus [1980] has formulated his deterministic hypothesis about natural language sentence parsing, the question may be raised as to whether the semantic interpreting algorithm that is contained in CASUS is or is not deterministic. Deterministic parsing is per definition such analysis which need never return from a wrong path, because it is able to decide beforehand which path is correct. Put in other words, deterministic parsing typically does not use backtracking, which is the deletion of already built syntactic structure. I am not convinced about the correctness of Marcus' hypothesis; in Van Bakel [1982] I tried to demonstrate that there exist certain natural language sentences which cannot be analyzed within a deterministic model. It has to be added, that even Marcus admits that at least semantic interpretation cannot be performed deterministically. A relevant point is also, that to correctly interpret an ambiguous sentence, an interpreter should return from it's first correct path to follow the second, also correct path, so, in order to detect ambiguities, an analyzer should typically not operate in a deterministic way. Whatever might be said about it, CASUS surely does not operate deterministically as is clearly shown by the example analysis that is displayed in the appendix.

I think it should be noticed that our model is not only suitable for my linguistic goals, but also incorporates a number of linguistically interesting questions which will be important in all application situations where automatic sentence analysis has to be performed in a not trivial way. The way analysis is performed is not trivial if no heavy constraints are laid upon the sentences to be analyzed. It may be pointed out that all of the analyzing and interpreting work that is done by AMAZON and CASUS, will also have to be done in such non-trivial situations, automatic translation not excluded. That is why the work might be considered to be of some importance as an experiment in automatic processing of Dutch. I am sure that the model AMAZON–CASUS, also in it's present state with shortcomings still adhering to it, gives a good view on the complexity of linguistic analysis.

At several places below, formal descriptions are given of certain datastructures, e.g. of the language SELANCA in section 3.1. The following (very informal) rules apply for the used notation:

(1) Rule IS
        left hand side of the rule ,
        defining symbol ,
        right hand side of the rule .
    Defining symbol IS : .
    Left hand side of the rule IS
        symbol .
    Right hand side of the rule IS
        alternatives followed by a point .
    Alternatives IS
        zero or more alternative .
    Alternative IS
        concatenation of symbols followed by a semicolon .
    Concatenation of symbols IS
        one or more symbol separated by commas .
    Symbol IS
        a string literal .

The tree structures that are shown on many places throughout the book are connected automatically with the program CASUS. For that reason they are presented in a divergent type. The program outputs those structures in the form of labeled bracketings, which are mapped into tree structures afterwards by the program ARBOR, written by Peter Arno Coppen. These trees are transferred to the text editor as to form part of the present study. It should be mentioned also that, as soon as the trees are being treated by CASUS, their diagrams do not show the original words of the sentence any more: they are replaced by the stem form of the lexical item they represent. The lexical semantic features and the features which result from the application of redundancy rules are never represented in the trees and in the final output the non splitting nodes are skipped.

## 1.2 A TWO-STAGE ANALYZING MODEL

The present section deals with the organization of the analyzer AMAZON - CASUS as a whole. Figure (1) shows the structure of the two-stage interpreter at it's highest level:

(1)

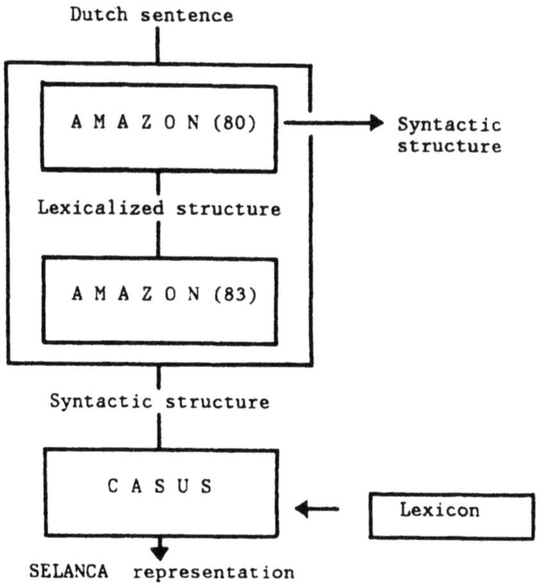


The main feature of the analyzing system is it's composition in two stages: a morphological, lexical and syntactic step, followed by a semantic step. The morphological analysis and lexical categorization is performed by the old modules built for that purpose in AMAZON(80). AMAZON(80) was, or rather is, mainly a syntactic parser in the form of a SNOBOL computer program. It yields a syntactic analysis of an input sentence. This structure, which is also indicated in the figure, is no longer important in the present situation, since the later developed AMAZON(83) has taken over the task. AMAZON(80) also produces a lexicalization of the sentence, which is to be analyzed syntactically by AMAZON(83). The resulting syntactic structure in the form of a labeled bracketing is input to the semantic interpreter CASUS. For details about the different states of AMAZON, the reader should refer to chapter 2. Of course it would be possible to distinguish three steps in the semantic analyzer as well. It is a matter of appreciation to consider the morphological and lexical analysis as a separate component beside the syntax or rather as a part of it. The figure shows that I prefer the latter idea. The main problem is not the border between morphology and syntax but the question whether to integrate or to separate syntax and semantics. In our model, the functions were spread over two separate components. It is quite easy to see, that it must be possible to integrate the syntactic analysis and the semantic interpretation in one system if it is possible to let them operate apart. Let us examine this question first.

Suppose that there exists consensus about what an adequate semantic representation of a natural language sentence should look like and that it has to be generated on the basis of some syntactic structure, assigned to the sentence by a surface syntax. There will be no doubt some grammar or computer program which could do the job. That grammar - let us confine ourselves to that - would have to express what the syntactic structure of the sentence should look like and how the meaning should be associated with that structure on the different levels. The input would be the sentence in it's primary form - say the words in character representation, delimited by blanks - and the output a representation of the sentence's meaning. Between input and output would be found a number of intermediate representations in a quantity that would depend on the number of different subsequent processes to which the sentence had been submitted. It would be arbitrary to draw the borderline which should separate syntax and semantics somewhere between two different subsequent intermediate representations. In other words, the semantic interpreting algorithm or grammar, would start with topics that are generally considered to be of syntactic nature and would end with specifications of a semantic kind, without leaving a possibility to draw an objective syntactic-semantic border. This can only be interpreted as: there is no principal difference between syntax and semantics.

This conclusion is heavily depending upon the situation that constrains it, viz. a computer model that assigns semantic representations to input sentences. However, there is a possibility for another approach. The basic observation that for somebody who does not understand a certain language it is absolutely impossible to make any sensible remark about even the most elementary syntactic organization of one of it's sentences, entails that also assigning syntactic structures to sentences is essentially a kind of semantic interpretation. Assigning structure to something cannot be anything else but saying something about it's meaning. A formal theory is characterized both by it's formalism and by it's interpretation. A formalism without an interpretation is a dead body; an interpretation without a formalism to be interpreted cannot be conceived of. If semantics is considered as an interpretation, it is obvious that no semantics may exist except one that operates on syntactic structure. The interpretation has to be of formal nature, just as it's object, the syntax. Ideally, the interpretation will obey a set of formal rules, which operate on formal syntactic structures. As syntactic structure is also the result of the application of formal rules, it is a rather arbitrary matter where to draw the borderline between the rules of syntax and those of semantic interpretation. It seems possible, when speaking of analyzing natural language sentences, to consider the work of the surface syntax, which assigns syntactic structures to rows of words, as a kind of interpretation too, albeit not of syntactic structure but of natural language sentences. The difference between syntax and semantics, or rather between formalism and interpretation, seems to be principally a matter of taste, depending on the way somebody wants to look at his own work[6].

From the previous paragraph it should not be concluded that the transparancy of the border between syntax and semantics is the eminent ground to build semantic analyzers containing just one component. The principal advocats of doing so, viz. most scholars in the environment of A.I. research, mainly use totally different arguments and the defenders of the opposite idea, e.g. the present author, do not base their conviction upon fundamental differences between syntax and semantics. As to the former, it may be noted that they consider (syntactic) analyzing of sentences as a semantic matter in principle. The difference between the notions parsable and interpretable should not exist. Syntax seems to be non existent in their view[7]. That is why a *semantic* grammar is being aimed at, in which e.g. no notion *noun phrase* exists but only *noun phrase which refers to an X* for every semantic category X in the domain. Semantic and syntactic knowledge, thus, totally coincide, which is not the same as saying that no absolute borderline exists between them. I think this view can be understood if the research is mainly aiming at modeling conceptual processes in human minds, rather than at natural language structures[8].

The choice in my case was for a two-stage analyzing model. A basic thought in favour of this was the observation that also for a native speaker with little theoretic linguistic concern, it is possible to abstract from the actual words used in a particular sentence and to identify what may be called the syntactic structure. This structure is not to be considered as a theoretical artifact but has an empirical state. It may be concluded, that a theory with a rather abstract structure as it's starting point is not to be discarded as insufficiently motivated from a psychological point of view. More important still for the choice was the following idea. A model of understanding natural language sentences should not only be adequate as to the native speaker's intuitions that it should reflect, but also show a clear structure as a linguistic theory, characterized by the fact that different levels should appear in accordance with different theoretical levels. From a merely theoretical point of view, it should reflect all possible significant generalizations. A model that should mix things that are to be distinguished on theoretical grounds is to be rejected. This theoretical concern seems to be in full parallel with ease of working, while developing the computer model. It is possible to deal with the form of a sentence without being obliged to take into account from the very beginning certain lower level details. It is a general experience that it is difficult enough to account for all facts that are relevant on a certain level, even when having the possibility to let less important things wait. It does not make sense, moreover, to distinguish e.g. a number of semantic subcategories of nouns, without dealing with the category noun in general, if this should be possible. Whatever may be said about the relations between syntax and semantics, there is a principal difference between e.g. the structure and the semantic contents of a sentence like *Colorless green ideas sleep furiously*. That difference has to be shown by the model. The only way is to distinguish different theoretical levels, like is done with AMAZON and CASUS. In my configuration, AMAZON represents the general knowledge of Dutch surface structures and CASUS the semantic knowledge.

There is another reason to choose for an analyzer consisting of two components, i.e. the difference between contextfree language phenomena and others. The question as to which phenomena can and which cannot be accounted for by a contextfree grammar is a point of discussion nowadays. Although Gazdar [1979] is of a different opinion, it is clear that not all natural language structures are contextfree. The structure $a^n b^n c^n$ for instance (a certain number of occurrences of *a*'s, followed by the same number of *b*'s and the same number of *c*'s) is of that kind and does appear in natural languages[9]. Only a certain part of the phenomena to be described can be dealt with by a contextfree grammar. As to the rest, another instrument will have to be looked for. In the AMAZON-CASUS model, the contextfree features are accounted for in the first component, whereas the others are dealt with by CASUS. It has to be pointed out, that, in this connection, it is not of great importance whether the phenomena to be touched upon are really contextfree in the strictly theoretical sense of the word. It is well-known, that in linguistic description, where clarity is such an important feature of the descriptions used, certain structures are accounted for by transformational rules, although a contextfree approach would do. An example in point is the separation of a verb into two parts in Dutch (see section 3.2.1.4). In order to reduce the number of rules, it is easier to define a separate syntactic node for both parts and restore the verb's unity afterwards in a transformational way. When I say that contextfree matters are dealt with by AMAZON and the others by CASUS, I refer to these cases. This approach is a very common way of working in linguistics. All theories with a main concern for generalization, build a syntax that is too tolerant and defines a great number of ungrammatical structures, which will have to be filtered out by some second instrument. In our case, AMAZON accepts quite a lot of ungrammatical Dutch sentences, which are to be discarded by CASUS.

# 2
# The Surface Syntax Amazon

In this chapter we deal with the syntactic analyzer AMAZON. For explanation purposes it will be necessary to refer now and then to one of the three different states AMAZON has passed through. Using the name AMAZON without any special reference we refer to the syntactic analyzer in it's present form. In cases where reference should be made to earlier forms we use the indications AMAZON(75) and AMAZON(80). Also the indication AMAZON(83) is used now and then for the present form. The older forms were reported in Van Bakel [1975] and Van Bakel [1981] respectively. AMAZON(83), which was developed by Jenny Cals, will be reported in connection with a project that has not been finished yet.

Section 2.1 deals with the morphological analyzer and the lexicon which are to be used in connection with AMAZON(83). These components are embedded in the old AMAZON(80), as will be explained. Section 2.2 gives some information about the syntax strictly speaking.

It is the function of the surface syntax to assign syntactic labels to all parts and subparts of the sentence, in order to yield a description that is sufficiently rich to be the basis for a more detailed interpretation which has to follow. The syntax need not be adequate in all respects. If this would be aimed at, it would become a large and lazy machine, lacking all transparancy and simplicity. If it would cause an error somewhere, it would be a huge job to debug it, and if it would be correct in all details, it would already be itself a semantic interpreter. Just the fact, that we decided to work in two separate steps, implies that the syntax is only a first, rather rough tool, which leaves a lot to be done in second instance.

To give an idea of the way Dutch sentences are structured by AMAZON, I give a short summary of the grammar. As the intention is to give a global impression, this survey will not be correct in all respects. The reader should compare the information with the the full grammar in the appendix. The symbols used are the same and can easily be looked up. The numbers added refer to the indices in the appendix.

(1) (75) SE : eerste , VC .
(15) eerste : CC ; BW ; PC ; NC ; AJ ; W1 ; W2 ; W3 ; W4 ; W5 .

| | |
|---|---|
| (90) | VC : PV , MI , CL , UL . |
| (133) | PV : finite verb . |
| (32) | MI : middle parts . |
| (16) | CL : cluster of verbs . |
| (89) | UL : CC ; W1 ; W2 ; W4 ; W5 ; PC . |
| (46) | NC : LW , NA , NK , NP . |
| (51) | NA : W2 ; W4 ; W5 ; TW ; AJ . |
| (54) | NK : noun . |
| (58) | NP : PC ; W1 ; W2 ; W4 ; W5 . |
| (62) | PC : VZ , NC . |
| (102) | Wi : MI , CL , UL . (i = 1...5) |
| (95) | CC : VW , W1 . |
| (2) | AJ : adjective . |
| (10) | BW : adverb . |
| (86) | TW : numeral . |
| (29) | LW : article . |
| (64) | VZ : preposition . |
| (98) | VW : conjunction . |

This syntax has a simple structure. The way details are included in it (as shown in the appendix) makes it rather powerful. Not too many analyses are produced and the analyses that are produced are quite suitable to be used for semantic interpretation. I realize, that the reader should still perform some investigation himself in order to become acquainted with the grammar.

## 2.1 THE MORPHOLOGY AND THE LEXICON OF AMAZON

The grammar AMAZON as it is shown in section 1 of the appendix does not contain real Dutch words as terminals. The deepest rules are of the following type:

(1) n0 : "N0" , "(" , woord0 , ")" .

(See rule 149). The symbol *woord0* is rewritten as a string of *letter0*'s (See rule 157). The linking of certain Dutch words with a lexical symbol like *woord0* takes place under AMAZON(80). As was mentioned above, AMAZON in it's first version was developed in 1975. In that form it was a SNOBOL computer program, consisting mainly of a number of morphological subroutines, a number of syntactic functions and a component to do the administration. The morphological subroutines were operating as deepest functions of the syntax. In a later form of AMAZON, when the morphological functions were separated, they operated once for all words of a sentence, transforming it into a string of lexical symbols. Rebuilding AMAZON into a contextfree affix grammar we had to choose to include in it a great number of morphological and lexicalizing rules, or to leave them out. The former would require a very large number of rules indeed that would slow down heavily the parsing process and at the same time deprive AMAZON of it's nice flexibility. The 1975 and 1980 versions both had a dynamic lexicon: meeting an unknown word, the interactive program would ask the user to define it. That fine facility would disappear totally without any compensation. We decided, therefore, to choose the latter, being compelled in that way to use the old morphological components of AMAZON.

A lot of changes on the syntactic level have been introduced into AMAZON since the time it was developed first, very few, however, concerning the morphology and the lexicalization. Thus, to comment on these parts of AMAZON(83), I may repeat by and large what was already reported in Van Bakel [1975].

1. The Verb.

The morphological analyzer of AMAZON is able to associate all different forms of the regular (weak) verb with the form of the 1st person singular present tense. For this is used a rule like (2):

(2) stem forms :
stem form ;
stem form , "e" ;
stem form , "en" ;
stem form , ("de" ; "te") ;
stem form , ("den" ; "ten") .

The stem form has to be defined in the dynamic lexicon. This can be done interactively, occasionally after the program has sent a message that word so and so is not known to the system. The knowledge to associate e.g. *maken* and *stappen* with the lexical forms *maak* and *stap* respectively is also present in the morphological analyzer. This function, that doubles the vowel and singles the consonant, is also used in connection with nouns, where the same phonological or, for that matter, spelling relations exist. Once a certain stem form has been defined in the lexicon, the morphological analyzer is able to associate it with compound verb forms. On the basis of e.g. *haal* also *neerhalen*, *afhaalde*, *opgehaald* etc. can be identified as verbal forms.

It should be noticed that irregular (strong) verb forms are defined in the morphological analyzer in an ad hoc way.

Since the syntax AMAZON is not interested in agreement or tense correspondences, the different verb forms are not formally characterized as, say, 1st person singular present tense, 3rd person plural past tense etc. These semantic aspects of sentence structure, as they may be considered, are only treated in the semantic analyzer CASUS. We will return to that matter below.

2. The Noun

The morphologic alternation of the noun is quite minimal in Dutch. The analyzer is able to distinguish a plural on *-en* and *-s* when the singular form is defined in the lexicon. On the other hand, there are quite a lot of derived nouns that are recognizable by certain suffixes: *-enaar*, *-nier*, *-nis*, *-iaan*, *-isme*, *-ment*, *-schap*, etc. They are all recognized by AMAZON(80).

3. The Adjective.

More or less the same rules are used in connection with the adjective as are with the noun. There is only one inflectional form that is present in an associating rule, viz. the form on *-e*. On the other hand, there exist, also in connection with the adjective, a great number of derived forms, such as on *-baar*, *-loos*, *-isch*, *-zaam*, *-ig*. It is clear that the rule that associates forms like *maak* and *maken*, *stap* and *stappen*, is also to be used in connection with derived adjectives.

4. Numerals

Numerals also are built more or less in accordance with morphological rules. The analyzer under AMAZON does, however, not deal with the subject in an interesting way. Numerals are defined as strings of digits, occasionally extended with the suffix *-de*, *-e* or *-ste* to build ordinals.

Undefined numerals are also known to the analyzer: *weinig* (few), *veel* (many), *genoeg* (enough) etc. and the undefined ordinals *eerste* (first), *laatste* (last) etc.

5. Adverbial pronouns

In Dutch syntax there is a word category with few members but rather interesting syntactic properties, viz. the adverbial pronouns like: *daarmee*, *hierdoor*, *waarvan*, *erop*. The most striking feature of these is the possibility to appear separated, e.g.

(3)
Daar luister ik niet naar.
(There listen I not to)

For AMAZON, this separation is out of order. The morphological analyzer is only able to recognize the composed forms mentioned. The separated parts represent separated lexical categories, the first part being an adverb and the second an AV.

Other word categories of Dutch do not show inflection. The members are defined ad hoc. Since these word classes are closed, no facility is needed to add new members to them. The dynamic lexicon of the AMAZON morphological analyzer is therefore restricted to the classes of verbs, nouns and adjectives.

6. Lexical categories

In (4) I give a short characterization of all lexical categories of AMAZON(83). I refer to the lexical rules in section 1 of the appendix.

| | | |
|---|---|---|
| (4) | VSUBPO | main verb of a clause the form of which is finite verb. |
| | VSUBTIO | main verb of a clause the form of which is *te*+infinitive. |
| | VSUBIO | main verb of a clause the form of which is an infinitive. |
| | VDWO | main verb the form of which is past participle. |
| | TDWO | main verb the form of which is present participle. |

| | |
|---|---|
| HVTIPO | auxiliary claiming *te*+infinitive, the form of which is finite verb. |
| HVTITIO | auxiliary claiming *te*+infinitive, the form of which is *te*+ infinitive. |
| HVTIIO | auxiliary claiming *te*+infinitive, the form of which is infinitive. |
| HVTITDO | auxiliary claiming *te*+infinitive, the form of which is present participle. |
| HVTPO | auxiliary claiming generally a past participle, the form of which is finite verb. |
| HVTTIO | auxiliary claiming generally a past participle, the form of which is *te*+infinitive. |
| HVTIO | auxiliary claiming generally a past participle, the form of which is infinitive. |
| HVTTDO | auxiliary claiming generally a past participle, the form of which is present participle. |
| HVIPO | auxiliary claiming an infinitive, the form of which is finite verb. |
| HVITIO | auxiliary claiming an infinitive, the form of which is *te*+infinitive. |
| HVIIO | auxiliary claiming an infinitive, the form of which is infinitive. |
| HVITDO | auxiliary claiming an infinitive, the form of which is present participle. |
| NO | noun. |
| ADJO | adjective. |
| BWO | adverb. |
| RELADVO | interrogative or relative adverb: *waar* hij woonde . |
| GRADVO | adverb of grade: *erg* zwart (very black). |
| ADVPRTO | adverbial part of separable (separated) verb. |
| LWO | article. |
| QUODO | interrogative or relative pronoun, not in attributive use: *wie* binnenkwam (who came in); *die* binnenkwam. |
| QUISO | interrogative or relative pronoun in attributive use: *welke* man vertelde ... (which man said ...). |
| ATTRIPRO | (another) pronoun in attributive use: *deze* man (this man); *mijn* boek (my book). |
| PRONO | pronoun (not yet mentioned). |

| | |
|---|---|
| VRZO | preposition. |
| RTELWO | ordinal. |
| HTELWO | numeral. |
| GRVGWO | grammatic conjunction: *of* (whether), *dat* (that). |
| NVGWO | coordination conjunction. |
| VGWO | (other) conjunction. |

## 7. Ambiguities

For the morphological analyzer two types of ambiguities exist, viz. 1 the word form met may have to be associated with two different lexical entries e.g. *weg* (way, away) may be an adverb or a noun; 2 the word form met may receive different syntactic functions, e.g. *dat* (that) may be a demonstrative pronoun, a relative pronoun and a conjunction. The differences between the first case and the second are not so big as one would possibly think. It seems to be rather arbitrary to consider *weg* as an occurrence of different lexical items and *dat* as an occurrence of one and the same item with different syntactic values. In connection with *weg* also it seems possible to consider the occurrences as variants of one lexical item and, the other way round, *dat* as a form of different lexical items. The morphological analyzer deals with these words in very much the same way. The old version of 1975 started parsing a sentence with a certain hypothesis about the function of an ambiguous word. When the analysis failed, the user had the opportunity to try the next hypothesis the analyzer had detected. The total number of possible tries was the product of the ambiguity factors of all the ambiguous words in the sentence. Since this approach involved quite a lot of waiting time for the user (while he was continuously thinking of the correct combination that he already knew), we started soon to give the user the opportunity to put in front the hypothesis he preferred. It was only a little step from that point to the way AMAZON(80) works: the morphological analyzer gives a message about a detected ambiguity, together with an enumeration of the possible interpretations and the user is asked what he might choose. Since the morphological analyzer for the present form of AMAZON was not changed, it is still the way things happen. It is my opinion that it is theoretically irrelevant that the parser is not confronted with all combinations of possible interpretations for ambiguous words. The difference is merely quantitative[10].

To show how the ambiguities are treated by AMAZON(80) I give a sample tracing of the interaction of the morphological analyzer and the user in section 5 of the appendix.

On the background AMAZON(80) produced the following input for the syntax AMAZON(83):

(5) HVTPO(HEB)PRONO(JE)ATTRIPRO(ZIJN)NO(BOEKEN)VDWO(MEEGE-BRACHT).

## 2.2 THE SYNTAX OF AMAZON

The adequacy of a syntax of a natural language can only be tested by using it in some way or another. An analyzing syntax should prove it's qualities while analyzing sentences. It is almost impossible to get a correct idea of the way it reflects a speaker's intuitions by only looking at a formal notation or, for that matter, by testing by heart whether certain types of sentences are predicted correctly. This is a cause of real problems when one intends to give an idea of a grammar's descriptive power. Therefore we must restrict ourselves to some impressions. The affix grammar AMAZON(83) as a whole is shown in the appendix.

There is a lot to say about technical aspects of the grammar. In the form we present it below it is a contextfree affix grammar. It contains two parts: the production rules and the meta-grammar. The production rules are recognizable by the production symbol ":". The meta-rules show a double colon "::" as production symbol. The meta-rules specify the way the affixes of the production rules have to be substituted to obtain the grammar in it's final form. Every production rule has as many counterparts in the final form of the grammar as amounts the product of the meta-rule interpretation possibilities of it's affixes. If a production rule contains two affixes and the meta-grammar specifies for them 2 and 3 possible interpretations respectively, 6 rules in the final grammar will result. An interpretation chosen for an affix at one place in a production rule has to be chosen for all occurrences of that affix in the rule. See (1):

(1) X<featurea,featureb> : Y<featurea> , Z<featureb> .
featurea :: "p" ; "q" .
featureb :: "A" ; "B" .

Will yield:

X<pA> : Y<p> , Z<A> .
X<qA> : Y<q> , Z<A> .
X<pB> : Y<p> , Z<B> .
X<qB> : Y<q> , Z<B> .

Since all the rules of the grammar are contextfree and since the production by the meta-rules yields a finite set of interpretations for the affixes used, the resulting grammar will be finite and contextfree. Therefore, the way the grammar is written, is only a shorthand notation for that resulting grammar.

Before being transformed into a contextfree parser by the parser generator of Ir. Hans Meijer (department of Computer Science, KUN University Nijmegen), the grammar has to be blown up according to the conventions just mentioned. The program used for that purpose is BLOWUP, written by Peter Arno Coppen (department of Computational Linguistics, KUN). The process yields 233 production rules, with 472 rule right hand sides all together, containing 958 syntactic symbols.

The author of a grammar of a natural language has the intention to characterize a certain subset of the sentences of that language, ideally as many as possible. Since a natural language, as has been proved by Brandt Corstius [1974, 96], is not contextfree, it will be impossible to define all and only it's sentences by a contextfree grammar. The grammar will be too wide or too narrow. As a matter of fact, most grammars will show to be too wide and too narrow at the same time. AMAZON is too narrow in lacking a definition for e.g. all Dutch sentences that start as (2):

(2) Al is het ook ...
Al had Jan ook ...

It is too wide on the other side in accepting sentences like (3):

(3) * Jan dacht dat Karel Karel Karel het zei.

Another aspect of the inadequacy of AMAZON is the fact that it assigns unacceptable syntactic structures to certain sentences. Sentence (4)a e.g. is assigned the structures (4)b and (4)c:

(4) a. Hij vertelde de man die hij zag dat ik het gedaan had.
(He told the man whom he saw that I it done had)
b. (Hij vertelde (de man (die hij zag)) (dat ik het gedaan had))
c. (Hij vertelde (de man (die hij zag (dat ik het gedaan had)))

The construction *dat ik het gedaan had* is recognized as last part (UL) of two different verbal constructions. AMAZON lacks the semantic and/or syntactic knowledge needed for a correct decision. It is typically this kind of thing that forms the background of the problematic adequacy of contextfree grammars for describing natural languages. Problematic in that it is uncertain whether a contextfree grammar is an instrument powerful enough to describe these things.

What is needed to give a correct account of (4)a.? It is obvious that as regards the verbs *vertelde* and *gedaan* the subcategorization rules are violated in (4)c. *Vertelde* has only one NP with it and *gedaan* has one too many, because *die* has to be connected with this verb by rules of WH-movement if the clause whith *dat* is interpreted as an object of *zag*. Consequently, the grammar has to imply all this knowledge to discard the analysis. This means that the production rules should be controlled by semantic features of a verb. The syntax then should be possessed of quite a lot of lexical information. A more or less adequate production rule might run as (5):

(5) VP<age,dat,obj> : V<age,dat,obj> , NP<age> , NP<dat> ,
NP<obj> .

This notation however does not prevent ungrammatical sentences, since the semantic features claimed by a specific verb for it's, say, object are not specified. In addition to this, (5) is still lacking a specification of a possible local adverb, a possible causal subclause, a combination of these two, etc. It is obvious that the syntax has to be almost as detailed as the lexicon of the grammar. This is, if not theoretically reprehensible, a totally unworkable situation for the linguist, since it urges him to concentrate on every detail from the beginning and forbids him to hierarchically organize the developing of the model. For me, it was one of the reasons to choose a model in two separate components: a contextfree surface parser and a powerful semantic interpreter.

Not all of the syntactic structure that is defined in AMAZON(83) is used by CASUS to yield a semantic representation. What is used is only that part of the structure which is associated with syntactic labels that do not end with a zero, while the parts of the labels that appear between angle brackets are neglected. The neglected parts are nevertheless not meaningless. I will try to explain that. Consider one of both structures of sentence (6) as defined by AMAZON(83)[11]:

(6) Jan houdt van Marie
(John loves Mary)

first in (7) with full syntactic information and in a more slender figure afterwards in (8):

(7) S0
SE
eveerste0
eerste0

```
    NC<nietrelatief_0>
      evlw<nietrelatief>0
        empty0
      evna<0>0
        empty0
      NK<noun>
        n0
          N0 ........................................................ (Jan)
      evnp0
        empty0
      evcj<8>0
        empty0
VC<0>
  v<0>0
    PV
      VSUBP0 .................................................... (houdt)
    evcj<18>0
      empty0
  midden<0>0
    MI<0>
      mid<0>0
        middendelen<0>0
          middendeel<0>0
            PC<1>
              VZ
                vrz0
                  VRZ0 ...................................... (van)
              NC<nietrelatief_1>
                evlw<nietrelatief>0
                  empty0
                evna<1>0
                  empty0
                NK<noun>
                  n0
                    N0 .................................... (Marie)
                evnp0
                  empty0
                evcj<8>0
                  empty0
              evcj<15>0
                empty0
  evul0
    empty0
```

```
evcj<17>0
  empty0
```

In this figure, the production of the rules (157) and (158) (see below in section 1 of the appendix) is skipped.

```
(8) SE
      NC
          NK ........................................................... Jan
      VC
          PV ........................................................... houdt
          MI
                    PC
                        VZ ............................................. van
                        NC
                            NK ......................................... Marie
```

As will be clear, the reduction of a structure of type (7) to a structure of type (8) raises a question as to the relation between them. Since NC is a superset of the NC's of the rules (43), (44) and (46) of the grammar, it will be possible in principle to find one structure of type (8) on the basis of a number of different structures of type (7). However, since all rules belonging to the set NC differ from each other as to their internal structure, this will be impossible again. But in that case, it may be asked what is the meaning of the difference between the structures of type (7) and of type (8). The best answer to that question is, that the type (7) structures cover information that is merely dropped by the reduction to the type (8). As was pointed out above, the grammar AMAZON has passed through some evolution since 1975. Only in 1983 Jenny Cals succeeded in building *the same* grammar in a contextfree form[12]. In the meantime we started already building CASUS and so it was absolutely necessary to maintain in the context-free grammar to build all the syntactic structure on which CASUS was used to operate hitherto. As a matter of fact, we could have maintained juist the syntactic structures that are shown in (8), but in that case the grammar would have produced an unacceptable quantity of analyses. The constraints in the earlier SNOBOL-form of AMAZON(80), which excluded a great number of analyses algorithmicly on grounds that were not expressed in the syntax labels, had to be kept without adding new labels. The only way to do that was adding new labels and making them invisible in the output.

The parser that is generated by the system of Ir. Hans Meijer, is to be used in connection with a socalled analyzer, which specifies the way the output of the parser has to be represented. For the analyses shown in (7) and (8), different analyzers have been used in connection with one and the same generated parser.

I will try to give an impressionistic characterization of the power of AMAZON by commenting on certain rules. The choice I make cannot be but arbitrary. Reference to certain rules will be made by help of the sequence numbers which the production rules get in section 1 of the appendix. My remarks will be mainly repetitions of an earlier description. See [Van Bakel, 1984].

Rule (1) of the grammar only denotes the real initial symbol SE. The main rule of the grammar is (75):

(75) SE : eveersteO , VC<x> , evcj<"17">0 .

The first symbol after the colon means 'an occasional first part' (defined by rule (76) and further by (15)). It is worth noting that all syntactic symbols starting with *ev-* (which is to be associated with the Dutch word *eventueel*, occasional) concern parts that may be absent; they may produce an empty string. The VC in (75) has a parameter 'x'. It is a means for controling the interdependency between the way the finite verb is realized (the rules (67) and following and (133)) and the filling of the verbal endcluster (Cl, also parameterized; see the rules (16) up to (23)). In the earlier forms of AMAZON the computation of the raising and dropping of expectations about verbal forms on the basis of the actual verb forms met in the sentence could be performed by a piece of computer program that was embedded in the subroutine that recognized the cluster. In the contextfree form of AMAZON things work differently. Now the possible combinations of verbal forms have to be enumerated in an ad hoc way. See the rules defining the CL, mentioned above.

The last symbol of (75) means an occasional conjunction construction i.e. a possible coordination. Rules with CJ<-> occur frequently in the grammar. The affix causes the selection of a correct constituent to be coordinated with (or rather subordinated to) the construction of which CJ<-> is a part.

Hans Meijer's parser generator in it's present state does not admit left recursion. The point where a grammar of Dutch has to face that problem is situated in the NC: an NC may start with an NA (a premodifying constituent) that may be a verbal construction (W2, W4 or W5), that contains a middle part (MI) that may contain an NC as it's first part. See a construction like (9)

(9) de vissen verschalkende reigers
(the fishes catching herons)

In the present grammar the problem has been solved by an implementation of pseudo left recursion. The NC is provided of an affix to control the depth of embedding. The intention is to prevent deeper embeddings than level x. In normal Dutch sentences no deeper embeddings will occur than in (9) e.g. One more embedding will yield a rather unacceptable (however not ungrammatical) sentence:

(10) de water happende vissen verschalkende reigers
(the water biting fishes catching herons)

Both the NC<relatief> and the NC<nietrelatief> (see the rules (44) and (46)) have an affix '0tm2' (meaning: 0 up to and including 2). According to meta-rule (XIII) this yields three rules, i.e. with left hand side NC<0>, NC<1> and NC<2>. Expansion of NC<0> will cause the use of the same affix "0" (in rule (44) e.g.) for evna<0> (an occasional premodifying constituent). Via the rule 50, 51, 52, 53, 114, 34, 35, 33 and 39 the affix is passed to 40, where it is incremented to "1": NC<nietrelatief, "1">. Another cycle through these rules brings the affix to level "2" of rule 42, where the nonexisting word "xxx" will cause a failure. In this way no deeper embeddings will be tested. Obviously, this procedure is an incorrect account of a native speaker's intuitions about the structure of a language like Dutch. A correct account however would prevent every analysis for the time being. It should be noticed that the restriction is a temporary one. As soon as the parser generator has been changed, the grammar can be adapted in an easy way.

The middle part of a verbal construction (MI; see the rules 32 and following) also requires some comment. The main problem in connection with this collection of constituents is the occurrence of a relative or a non relative first element. That is the meaning of the difference MI<relatief> opposite to MI<nietrelatief>. The verbal constituent under which MI appears is defined as consisting of three parts: a middle part MI, a verbal cluster CL and an occasional last part UL. See the rules for the subclause (W1, rule 103), for the construction with infinitive (W2, the rules 114 and 120), the construction with *te* plus infinitive (W3, rule 108), for the construction with past participle (W4, the rules 110, 116 and 121), and for the construction with present participle (W5, the rules 112, 118 and 122). Since the NC shows left recursion and this recursion circulates over the verbal constructions, these rules had to be parameterized to control the depth of embedding. This enlightens the use of the affix *0tm2*. In the second place it was necessary to distinguish the use of verbal constructions in a premodifying subconstituent of the NC (for this purpose the affix *nca* is used), as a postmodifier of the NC (for this the affix *np*) and as a last part (UL) of a verbal construction (for this the affix *ul*). This last affix gets the same interpretation as *np*, since the constructions show no formal differences in both contexts. That is why there is no different rewriting rule for e.g. W2<np> and W2<ul>. The MI-part of these constructions requires sometimes a relative or interrogative pronoun as it's first part. In addition, a constituent under MI may never have the form of a relative or interrogative pronoun if it is not the first MI-part. These claims are controlled by the different affixes. See rule 32 and 35.

Let us consider verbal constructions as parts of other constituents. According to their context, they are subject to different restrictions. In the first place there is the restriction for verbal constructions as premodifiers in the NC. See the rules 114, 116 and 118, where the affix *nca* is used to select special forms of the constructions for that special context. If the rules mentioned are traced in the grammar below, it shows that only the verbal cluster is an obliged part. This means that e.g. a present participle alone can play the role of a W5. In the same way a *te* plus infinitive can play the role of a W2 and a past participle that of a W4. This definition is necessary to distinguish these forms from those that are possible under the NP (postmodifier) of an NC and the last part (UL) of a verbal construction. According to the rules 89, 120 and 124 the constructions contain in these contexts necessarily a MI or an UL. Consider the constructions:

(11) een opmerking, gemaakt bij de persconferentie
(a statement made at the press conference)
een opmerking, door de president gemaakt
(a statement, by the president made)
* een opmerking, gemaakt
... een opmerking gehoord, gemaakt bij de persconferentie
... een opmerking gehoord, door de president gemaakt
*... een opmerking gehoord, gemaakt

Other restrictions are applicable in other contexts. As a realization of *eersteO* (rule 15), W2, W3, W4 and W5 may have the form defined in the rules 106, 108, 110 and 112.

One of the most interesting features of AMAZON is the way the verbal clusters are controlled. Nearly all possibilities of Dutch in this point are recognized and correctly structured. Besides, the correct functions of auxiliaries are specified. To be correctly analyzed and interpreted, a construction like (12)

(12) Als hij zou willen komen zou voorzien moeten zijn ...
(If he would want come should foreseen must be ... (should have been foreseen))

(with seven verbal forms together) requires a rather sophisticated grammar.

# 3

# The Semantic Interpreter Casus

In chapter 3, the main component of the two-stage semantic analyzer is discussed, namely the program CASUS. The chapter consists of two major parts, the first of which concerns the semantic language used to express the meanings of sentences: SELANCA. The second part, dealing with the translation from AMAZON to SELANCA, is divided into a first section which contains mainly questions of linguistic nature, and a second, which touches upon matters of computer representation and implementation.

Before I deal with the precise functions of the semantic interpreter, I would like to discuss it's actual form in my implementation, viz. a SNOBOL computer program. Why, if the surface syntax has developed from a computer program into a contextfree affix grammar that is transformed into a parser generator by some system, should not the same approach be chosen as regards the second component? In connection with that question, a number of things have to be considered. First, it should be realized, that a system that assigns meaning representations to syntactic structures of natural language sentences is mainly intended to associate a sentence of some language l′ with a sentence of another language l″. Whatever may be the kind of both languages concerned, the process will always be some kind of translation. The way the target code is selected might be trivial, for instance if it were chosen in an ad hoc way from a numbered set, when the same number has been assigned to a sentence of the source language as to it's counterpart in the target language, but it may also have some sophistication, e.g. when the translation is driven by structural features of the source language. Translation may be regarded as an automatic sentence generation in language l″ on the basis of the sentence structure of language l′. If the generation process has been defined as a function of an input structure, it may very well be considered as a transformation. The most important question will be then: what is the kind of that transformation? Could a simple one to one relation be established between the elements of the languages concerned? If the input is a tree structure, the output would also have to be a tree structure, showing no other differences than such that could be expressed by a simple transliterating grammar. As soon as deletions should be performed or simple moving, the relations would be more complicated. Obviously, the differences between l′ and l″ will have to be of this kind, since, if they were not, the target language would show the same information structure as the source language in relation with which it would be just a dialect with a different lexicon. A translation of that kind would be too weak since the distance between both languages would be too small to even speak of a translation. It is very clear that the structure of the target language has to differ from that of the source language on a major point. Although it seems to be rather arbitrary which features should be considered important enough to call a translation a translation, I would suggest that changing tree structures is necessary for that: the translation of l′ sentences into l′′ sentences has to be of a transformational kind in this sense that tree structures are changed.

The conclusion must be, that for defining relations between syntactic and meaning expressing structures, a transformational grammar is needed and, consequently, a transformational grammar parser generator to transform it. However, a linguist will have to wait for this parser generator to be developed somewhere, to have it developed himself or even to build it really on his own desk. Transformational parser generators with full mightiness exist only in abstract form in somebody's head: they cannot be built, since an instrument without constraints is impossible in a constrained world. Some restrictions will have to be chosen. When chosen, however, they may easily appear to be the wrong ones for a certain application. In spite of what everybody calls necessary, it is very rare that someone finds the instruments he needs, built by other people in accordance with his wishes, usable on his computer, obtainable directly etc. If a parser generator should be found, it will be constrained in some way and possibly be imcompatible with the things one wants to do with it. It may very well be the case that one does not know, which restrictions are and which are not wanted or necessary or tolerable in a certain situation, as long as the linguistic theory to simulate has not been examined in that light yet. It has to be added that, in order to know which restrictions should be chosen for a certain purpose, rather vast explorations will have to be undertaken. To cut it short: let us assume that the SNOBOL computer program CASUS is that exploration. The idea that grammars should not have the form of computer programs should not be the enemy of linguistic exploration. Certain computer programs are acceptable as formulations of linguistic theories, provided that they are transparant and meet the claim of maximal generality in the same way as grammars should do.

The functions of the semantic interpreter CASUS are to be characterized as a set of formal relations between structures that are output by AMAZON and socalled SELANCA-expressions. The aim of the present study is mainly to describe those functions and relations. The interpreting process is an algorithm by which a tree structure is changed and enriched, yielding one or more SELANCA-expressions on the basis of one AMAZON-structure.

## 3.1 THE SEMANTIC LANGUAGE SELANCA

In our model of understanding natural language sentences AMAZON reflects the ability of native speakers to understand the structure of a sentence, apart from the meaning of the words used in it. This ability obviously exists, since a native speaker is able to understand in some way a sentence filled with nonsense words. A classic item (see Reichling [1935, 347]) in this context is:

(1) De vek blakt de mukken

In one of the possible readings, this is clearly understood as:

(2) (S (NP De vek) (VP (V blakt) (NP de mukken)))

If this observation is correct, it is possible to make a distinction between understanding the syntactic surface structure of a sentence only and understanding all of it. The rest is partly determined by the meaning of words, but it is more than that, since understanding word meanings is embedded in understanding syntactic structure and understanding structure has also to do with recognizing movement, which is not accounted for by AMAZON. While AMAZON represents the former, CASUS is a model of the second and, as such represents the total meaning of the sentence. Of course, the way the meaning of a sentence is represented is based on a certain idea of what meaning is supposed to be. In this section I will have to deal with that subject and, more precisely, with the structure of the semantic language in which the meaning will be represented. It is impossible to acceptably account for a semantic language without amply discussing the meaning phenomenon. Though this study is not intended to be a theoretic semantic study but rather an account of the way a meaning theory is used in a computer model of understanding natural language sentences, it is necessary to deal to some extent with meaning theory in general.

First of all, a few principal remarks about meaning and meaning representation have to be made. Meaning has to be associated with a formal system whose interpretation it is. This rather redundant statement is of some importance, as opposed to the idea that, before a sentence has been generated, there should exist some *conceptual base* where it's contents, which is going to be it's meaning afterwards, resides[13]. Of course we will have to suppose that there is 'something' 'somewhere', out of which a sentence originates, but this idea is absolutely useless. Even if this is the case - and there is no reason at all to doubt it - it surely will be the case also, that that conceptual base is inaccessible for direct investigation and will only be representable by some theory that makes use of a formal language. With respect to that formal language it will have to be proved that it is independent of the object to be described, which means that it puts no illegal constraints on it. But it seems to be impossible to prove this, since the necessary condition would be that the conceptual base were independently accessible to investigation. Another also rather discouraging remark is the following. We have to establish from the beginning that it will be impossible to express the meaning of a certain token without using another token which is claimed to bear the same meaning, whereas this semantic identity cannot be proved. Meaning may only be represented in a meaning bearing form and is not available apart from the form that bears it. This obviously being the case, the discussion never will reach a totally acceptable ending, as it will always be possible for someone to doubt the meaning equality between the first and the second form. As to transporting meaning from one form into another or, for that matter, from one language into another, there will be no proof that it has been done correctly[14]. This remark can be made beforehand, and it needs no research to see that it is true. Another principal question about meaning is, whether it is possible indeed to represent the meaning of a token t′ by a token t″. In other words, is it possible that two different tokens have the same meaning? There is more than one answer to that question. One answer might be: yes, it is, for the English sentence *He is my father* has the same meaning as the Dutch sentence *Hij is mijn vader*; and another: no, it is not, at least not when natural languages are concerned, for a language is an interpretation of reality which is culturally and historically determined, rather than a reference to an objective reality, and every natural language embodies another interpretation system of reality[15]. The second answer is not to be invalidated and, as a matter of fact, it is a fairly good representation of my personal opinion. But clearly this answer is a total frustration of linguistics, since it makes it impossible to generalize about human language: if it is impossible to say that sentences of different languages have the same meaning, it will also be impossible to compare those languages, totally apart from building an explanatory theory about human language in general. That price is too high. Let us therefore opt for the first answer.

In spite of these remarks, my study should not be considered as a contribution to meaning theory or semiotics. What the reader should expect is an exposition of a certain view on meaning, together with a view on semantic interpretation, and an explanation how this is performed in the model described. Great differences appear to exist between the goals of linguists dealing with semantic analysis. In extreme cases, meaning theory is used to add information to a database by entering natural language sentences which contain that information, or to retrieve information from a database. To put it in another way: in order to manipulate reality or at least a model of reality. This may be called extreme cases by which even the borders of linguistics seem to be crossed, since it is the most pretentious way meaning theory can be used anyhow because no further possibilities exist. This having been reached, linguistics will lack any further application possibility. Mostly, however, the intentions of linguists are restricted and certainly mine are. I do not want a certain part of the world to be introduced within the research situation, as is the case in question answering systems and in much work of the Artificial Intelligence (A.I.) environment, because I want to stick to linguistic theory. As will be argued below, linguistics is passed when reality is reached. Connecting language and reality will not be the task of linguistics.

Like most problems also the meaning problem has a philosophic nature. It is not in the first place a practical problem that should be solved in a practical way, although in quite a number of studies with a linguistic or, mainly, A.I. character, this impression is given. Students of formal semantics have spent a lot of energy in efforts to solve the meaning problem by use of a logical formalism, since a logical analysis might be expected to give the best results. As everybody knows, however, logic has not led to a satisfying solution as yet. A necessary condition would be, that language obeys the laws of logic. If this should appear not to be the case, the undertaking would be deemed to fail beforehand. Only if the systems of language and logic were in full parallel, the effort would have a chance to be successful. Of course it will not be forbidden that a meaning representing language has some similarity with a logical calculus, but this may not constrain the language structures. If a logical calculus would seem to be a subset of a natural language or could be associated directly with such a subset, it would be an insufficient instrument. As a rule, a logical calculus is used to build expressions about some reality. In order to evaluate these, the reality has to be made available as part of some welldefined system. A system can never operate on objects which are not parts of it. If the set of objects about which true expressions should be generated or analyzed should show inconsistencies, the calculus would not be able to operate on them. The assumption while using a logical calculus is, that language speaks of a set of objects which can be defined exactly and in an objective way, and that this reality is a consistent system. I will show that this condition is not met and that, therefore, the effort must be a failure.

It has to be noticed first, that we should speak about reality in a non trivial way. We should not consider sentences in connection with which the problematic relation between language and reality should not be visible. It is tempting to say that there is no problem at all in that relation in a sentence like *The sun is shining*. If this would really be so, the sentence would not be a good example for the present discussion. I will argue, that, if there can be shown to be a problematic relation between language and reality in some instances, this should be regarded as a principal matter, which is also relevant as regards apparently unproblematic sentences.

Sentences do not only express what is the state of affairs, but often define or introduce or even *are* facts. This is shown by imperative sentences, which escape from the opposition true-false, and by socalled performative speech acts, e.g. a sentence like *I forbid you to go there*. If in a logical calculus a means would have to be built to establish their truth, one would have to create something that itself would be a model of the contents of the sentence, in order to let it function as a model of reality. A principal observation can also be made as regards the words *left* and *right*. It is a well-known and classic fact that there is no way at all to represent their meaning in another way than by these words themselves or by translations that are simply agreed upon to have the same meaning. It is not even possible to paraphrase them. This means that there exists no reality which is referred to by the words *left* and *right* except the meanings of these words themselves.

The main problem in analyzing the meaning of a natural language sentence within a logical calculus is the way reality has to be introduced in the system. Is there a way to objectively define or represent reality so that the contents of a sentence may be confronted with it in order to compute it's truth or falseness? The answer has to be negative, since, as can be shown, reality is not available outside a language system that represents it. Let us follow for a moment Jackendoff [1976 : 89] while dealing with the sentence *Fred is fat*. Jackendoff argues, that one of the claims made by the sentence *Fred is fat* is that the person designated by the name *Fred* is fat; the corresponding truth-condition is that the person is indeed fat. A formal theory of understanding meanings of sentences would have to be considered adequate if a sentence that is claimed to be true would be found to be in accord with some state of affairs in the world or with a state of affairs in a formal model of it. The confrontation of a sentence plus a meaning theory with reality is supposed to be part of an empirical test. Let us suppose some machinery could be built to perform the investigation. Without any doubt, knowledge about a person's fatness would have to be implemented in it in some way, which means that a kind of translation should be made of the concept of fatness into the hardware of the testing machine. But if this indeed is the case, it is no longer of any importance from a linguistic point of view whether or not Fred is fat. The main question would be no longer about the correctness of a meaning theory about the relation between a certain sentence and the corporeal condition of a person, but rather about the way the concept of fatness has been built into the machine or, put in other words, about the way the machine models the meaning of natural language. The question has been displaced. For an empirical test we should now look at this second relation. The investigation of Fred's condition has become a means to evaluate the correctness of a fatness measuring machine. Since testing whether a sentence is in accord with reality cannot be done without a machine, it is just as explanatory to say: the sentence is true if somebody else should say the same, or, even simpler: the sentence's truth condition is that the sentence is true. Formulating truth conditions is producing tautologies. When Barwise and Perry [1983] speak of *abstract situations* whose building blocks are individuals, properties, relations and locations, which are to be considered as *uniformities*, they build an interesting theory of meaning, which, however, is also directly depending upon the language system itself. If we call, for instance, one place *the same* as a second place, we refer to a set of objects in connection with which we want to consider it at a certain moment. These objects need not be totally identical, since they may have *changed*, neither will the absence of one of them be decisive for the use of the word *the same*. There is no way to absolutely specify which are the ultimate borders for using the word correctly. Every reality may be considered under infinitely many different aspects and it is depending upon the free choice of language only what is the actual reality spoken about.

To return to Jackendoff's argument, it is obviously important to note, that the word *fat* is not an image of reality but that the 'reality' of fatness is modelled into what it is by a concept in the human brain which is expressed in the language. The fatness is inconceivable without being expressed in some language. In this respect there is no difference in principle between *fat* and *left* or *right*. One may claim that the reality which is related to the word would not exist as such if it were not created by language[16]. Material reality is not absolute and objective. Suppose we ask somebody to describe as exactly as possible what should be considered to be a billiard-ball, and afterwards we inspect the cosmos and find an object in a spiral that is situated beyond Andromeda, which matches the description in all aspects. Everybody will agree, that the conclusion that the object is really a billiard-ball is incorrect, since the cultural interpretation is decisive. It is exactly this interpretation which is essential concerning the meaning problem. It is not reality which decides that something is or is not a billiard-ball: things we play billiard with are billiard-balls. This does not mean, that in physic reality (the way Fred's body is built up, what molecules are in it and in what quantities) things are different according to the way people speak about it. But it does mean, that by human language certain aspects of reality are selected and interpreted and that never two different sentences can be paraphrases in that they should describe the same reality[17]. Reality is unendlessly more complex than a certain sentence suggests. If a reality could be selected without a language, it would appear that in connection with it an unendless set of true sentences can be formulated and no one of these might claim to represent it adequately. That is the reason Simmons [1973] is mistaken in suggesting that there should be one and the same reality to be connected with the following sentence pair:

(3) John bought the boat from Mary.
Mary sold the boat to John.

Simmons tries to build a meaning (or rather knowledge[18]) representation that should be at the basis of both sentences, suggesting that there is one reality that is depicted in different ways in each one of them. There is no such reality that could be identified in an objective way to be in accord with both sentences or, for that matter, with one of them: no film camera could conclude to such thing nor whatever other machinery. Specifically cultural facts, like buying and selling, only exist by virtue of the human language that constitutes them and the same holds principally for all facts. If there were no language, buying and selling would be impossible. There is no ground, therefore, to postulate an autonomous reality that is referred to by natural language.

Computing a sentence's truth conditions has to meet still other severe difficulties. In Montague grammar meaning is represented by a logical formula which represents the conditions for a sentence to be true. The most significant shortcoming is that the system needs a rigid idea of reality. Formally, Montague semantics is based upon the principle of compositionality: the meaning of a construction is obtained by composing the meanings of it's parts. Every syntactic rule is accompanied by a semantic rule which specifies how to compute or formulate the meaning of the defined construction. The semantic rules are built according to a logical calculus, by which the meaning of the constructions is expressed, i.e. their truth conditions. This does not necessarily imply the claim to build a model of a certain world, in relation with which the sentence could be evaluated, but it does claim that there exists indeed something like an objective reality that has only to be inspected to see whether or not the sentence is true. Look at sentence (4): how should the reality be simulated in the system in correspondence with which the contents of this sentence has to be evaluated and how should the system operate with that sentence, if it is assumed that there is a model of the world built into the system:

(4) The ancients did not know that Hesperus was Phosphorus.

The ancients referred to the evening star and the morning star with these names respectively, being unaware of the fact that they were looking at one and the same planet of the solar system as we conceive it. If Hesperus and Phosphorus were one and the same object, sentence (4) should entail (5):

(5) The ancients did not know that Hesperus was Hesperus.

This is an unacceptable consequence and it seems to confront us with a rather fundamental problem. However, nobody would, I think, argue in the same way of the sentence

(6) Little Mary-Ann did not know that Santa Claus was uncle Henry.

saying that it should entail:

(7) Little Mary-Ann did not know that Santa Claus was Santa Claus.

The first mistake is to consider a name as a rigid pointer to a rigid object.Cfr. Kripke [1972]. This idea is not only a trivial matter but also obviously incorrect. Why should the concrete reality in the form of a certain human body, which might be associated trivially with the linguistic form *Santa Claus*, be of primary interest, when this linguistic form is compared with *uncle Henry*? Both of these linguistic forms are claimed to have the same extensional meaning. Both the name and the second indication are thus regarded as pointers to objects. It need hardly be argued that this interpretation entails that all indications of a certain object would have the same meaning, which seems to be an unacceptable conclusion, if it were only by it's suggestion that reference can only be made to material objects. I reject the interpretation since I consider it to be an instance of trivial materialism. The extensional meanings of linguistic forms differ in the same way as they do intentionally. Likewise, in the reality of the ancients, two different magnificent phenomena exist, one shortly after sunset and the other one, very similar of brightness, shortly before dawn. It makes no sense to connect these experiences with what modern astronomy has to say about it. I think, sentence (4) is true nor false, but simply nonsense and as such does not entail (5). Two different realities are mixed up in it, the one of which modern astronomic theory is speaking and the other in which the ancients lived. The way both realities are mixed is rather tricky and creates a sham problem, by suggesting the existence of one objective reality. Why should the world of modern astronomic theory be an objective reality, the only one that could be the universe of discourse with which the thoughts and utterances of the ancients should be related? Totally apart from the fact that modern astronomy is not to be identified with reality or with truth - it does not even make sense to raise that question, since truth and reality are functions of language - the astronomic truth about Hesperus and Phosphorus according to modern theories cannot be the universe of discourse for the ancients talking about certain phenomena in their firmament and consequently cannot determine the meaning of their words Hesperus and Phosphorus. Hesperus and Phosphorus were, in the world of the ancients, totally different phenomena. Of course, it is possible for us to speak about the ideas of the ancients in relation with ours, but we should be aware of the fact that this is done in an obscured way by sentence (4). This should run, to be explicit, as follows:

(8) The ancients did not know that, according to astronomic theories of later times, one and the same object is to be associated with the two different phenomena, referred to by them with the names Hesperus and Phosphorus.

The difficulties are clearly caused by a couple of unjustifiable restrictions about reality. It is incorrect to regard reality as one absolute and objective system. As sentence (4) shows, one sentence may have to be connected with different realities which are incompatible and mutually inconsistent. The conclusion must be, that there exists no absolute reality that should form the universe of discourse to contain both the thoughts and ideas of the ancients and our opinions and concepts, and even that there exists no absolute reality at all. If it is impossible to indicate a reality which should be considered as *the* reality, it is impossible at the same time to speak of meaning in terms of such a reality. By lack of an objective reality, it is impossible to use the socalled truth conditions of a sentence. Whithin the boundaries of linguistics it is senseless to speak of a sentence's truth condition, since nothing can be clarified by that.

Whereas the foregoing pages seem to characterize sufficiently what I am thinking of while speaking of meanings of sentences, things have not been described in very positive terms as yet. Let me try to indicate what will have to be understood by meaning in the context of the semantic interpreter CASUS. Language h to be viewed as as an historically and culturally determined interpreting theory of reality. Reality is the universal mystery in which mankind is living and language is the way this is available to humans. Reality may have an autonomous state of itself, but this is irrelevant, since it is only accessible for us in the way it appears within our minds and brains, that means within our language. The information that is coded in reality is decoded by language. It is impossible to verify the truth of a sentence directly, i.e. without investigating what language tells about reality. From a linguistic point of view it makes no sense to distinguish truth and affirmation.

Every sentence of a natural language has to be understood as the application of an interpreting theory to a certain part of reality. Somebody using sentence (6) refers with the word *Santa Claus* to a human-like being, playing a certain role in a certain situation, and characterized by the fact that children interpret his acting in a different way than adults do; and with *uncle Henry* to another social role, associated with historical facts of birth and education situations.

Specifying the meaning of a linguistic form is impossible without defining all meanings of all forms of the same language, and defining all of a certain language will have to imply defining all of the structure of reality. The phenomenon 'Santa Claus' has to be characterized in order to define the meaning of the word *Santa Claus*, since the reality that is indicated mainly with the word *Santa Claus* exists in a set of concepts which can only be represented in certain words. It is often suggested that for automatic translation all knowledge of reality should have to be built into the translating system; I think it is more correct to claim that in order to describe what we call reality, it is needed to fully describe language. What is considered to be impossible, typically regards human language rather than reality. If it should really be impossible what is being aimed at, the trouble originates in language itself.

All thoughts and opinions formulated in the previous pages have been important for the way the semantic language SELANCA has been designed. No try whatever was made to honour reality in another way than language honours it. My claim is, that this has led to a linguistically adequate semantic representation. The main idea behind the language is, that a meaning representation of a natural language sentence has to meet two claims: 1. the formalism used must be adequate to reflect all semantic information and no more than that, that is linguistically relevant and 2. it should reflect as little as possible of the language typical way the meaning is coded in the natural language in question. Between the Scylla and the Charibdis of these two claims, the semantic language of CASUS (SELANCA) is characterized as follows:

(9) SELANCA expression :
    semantic kernel ( arguments ) .
  semantic kernel : [ constituent + semantic function ] .
  constituent : V ; A ; N.
  semantic function :
    Proposition ;
    Agentive ;
    Dative ;
    Objective ;
    Factitive ;
    Instrumental ;
    Locative ;
    Attribute .
  arguments :
    argument ;
    argument , arguments ; .

argument :
operator ;
SELANCA expression .
operator :
adverbial constituent .

In the definition of the SELANCA expressions, the semantic kernel is followed by a number of arguments, placed between brackets. The meaning of the brackets is a subordination. The arguments are to be considered as nodes which are dominated by the semantic kernel. Square brackets are used in the definition of a semantic kernel, to indicate that it is an ordered pair: a constituent with a related semantic function. The functionname *Proposition* is meant to indicate the semantic function of a semantic kernel on the highest level of the sentence. We will return to these points instantly. The arguments of a semantic kernel are defined as a set of zero or more constituents, which can be operators or SELANCA expressions. An operator is an adverbial constituent, which means an adverb, a PC that is optional in that it is not claimed by subcategorization rules, or a conjunction construction, giving information about the time when, the place where, the reason why etc. the event or the act that is indicated by the semantic kernel occurred or was performed[19].

There are some relations between the language SELANCA and other representations of natural language meanings. Mainly it is Fillmore [1968] who was the stimulus for us to design SELANCA, but some lines also can be drawn to Jackendoff [1972]. Fillmore's case grammar defines a proposition as a verb connected with a set of case categories. At the deepest level of representation there appears a verb as a kind of semantic nucleus that controls the generation of the sentence. It is worth of note, however, that there are some significant differences between Fillmore's approach and ours. Fillmore's theory has not been used as a guide to build something like a sentence's deep structure. We do not generate deep structures but build semantic interpretations of sentences that in principle are taken for granted, whithout dealing with questions as to which sentences have the same deep structure, what should be considered to be really the deep structure of a certain sentence etc. We try to formalize a theory about the meaning of sentences, concluding occasionally that two sentences have the same meaning or that one sentence has different meanings, being inspired, while doing that, by Fillmore's concept of meaning. For the same reason, our work has little connection with the discussion about interpretative versus generative semantics[20]. Interpretative semantics is characterized by an autonomous syntax, by which the sentence structures are generated, and an independent interpretative component which specifies their meanings. Generative semantics has put forward the idea that the meaning of a sentence should not be the result of interpretation of an autonomously generated deep structure, but rather that syntax and semantics should form a single system of rules converting semantic into surface syntactic representations by a series of intermediate steps. Interpretative semantics seems to necessarily imply the viewpoint that syntax can be thought of without any reference to meaning and is therefore obviously objectionable, since it seems to totally deprive syntax of it's ultimate sense: the explanation of the meaning phenomenon. However, also the better of both approaches with respect to this, I mean McCawley's, seems to be inadequate. Just as the interpretative theory, also generative semantics is mainly concerned with the way a sentence is produced: it explains how a certain concept or thought is formulated in a sentence. That concept, in the form of a semantic representation, is operated upon by the grammar until finally the surface form of the sentence is reached. It is an important aspect of this theory that it suggests that the meaning of a sentence is something essentially metalinguistic, being the semantic representation an object that is introduced in the theory before the generation of the sentence strictly speaking is starting[21]. If a semantic representation (of what?) should be introduced before sentence generation starts, this seems to be possible only by using some kind of syntax which generates semantic representations, in connection with which the same question about the syntactic or semantic primacy can be raised.

In the context of the AMAZON-CASUS analysis I need not solve this problem, because I am not engaged in defining sentences. What the model simulates is the understanding of a natural language sentence which is taken for granted. Therefore I need not choose between interpretative and generative semantics, though my model in this respect is interpretative rather than generative. Thus, I need not suggest at all where sentences originate, whether their concept is primary to their syntactic form or the other way round.

Let us look to the above mentioned claims in somewhat more detail. As will be doubted by nobody, linguistically relevant semantic information is typically the information that is encoded in the sentence. All information is out of order which has no means of expression in the sentence. It is quite a problem what information has to be considered present in the sentence and how it should be represented outside of it. A question of principal importance is that about the status of lexical items: should lexical items be avoided in a semantic representation, as Jackendoff [1976] claims, or, rather, should they be kept because of their relevance for the way reality is structured by language. It will not surprise the reader, that I am inclined to choose the latter point of view. Certainly, they are language specific, but in order to honour the way reality is presented by an actual language it seems to be obligatory to respect them. Many scholars argue for lexical decomposition, not only in the field of A.I.

but also in linguistics. What is put in their place seems to be a set of lexical items on a lower level. This can be illustrated by a quotation from Wilks [1977], who gives a good idea of the way A.I. scholars tackle the problem, pointing out some differences between a number of authors. According to his sketch, Colby and Charniak share the opinion that semantic representation of natural language can be *by means of itself*, but Schank and Wilks prefer some *reduced, or primitive, representation*. The question indeed regards the way word meanings are to be represented. What Wilks is aiming at himself is shown by a representation of the verb *to drink* in (10):

(10) ((* ANI SUBJ) ((FLOW STUFF) OBJ) (SELF IN) ((THIS (* ANI (THRU PART))) TO) (MOVE CAUSE))

Wilks explanation reads: this sense of *drink* is being expressed as a causing to move a liquid object (FLOW STUFF) by an animate agent, into that same agent (containment case indicated by IN, and formula syntax identifies SELF with the agent) and via (direction case) an aperture (THRU PART) of the agent (Wilks [1977, 371]). Jackendoff [1976], though not a representative of the A.I. approach, comes rather near to this and also Simmons's way of lexical decomposition by describing all verbs with a set of five features: GO(), BE(), STAY(), CAUSE() and LET().

It may be clear already that I am not an advocate of lexical decomposition, nor, for that matter, of the A.I. approach of semantic analysis. Lexical decomposition as in (10) is a way of not taking seriously the forms whose meanings are to be represented. The result of the decomposition is merely going down a step from a ladder of unknown length. The new situation shows new basic forms, which are no less problematic than the earlier ones. Why, for instance, should the item FLOW not be decomposed into MOVE as a FLUID MASS, or something like that? As long as no theoretical arguments may be offered in favour of the approach, I am not enthusiastic for this kind of representation. Since meaning representation can but hope to make use of a system which lacks every necessary connection between tokens and their meanings, I think no principal improvement is to be expected. Why then the forward escape into a new set of even less usable symbols? Another reason to moderate the enthusiasm for an A.I.-like approach is that it's motivation is a possibility to manipulate a world rather than linguistic theory. Although the motivation of formal linguistics is the application of theoretical insights in concrete circumstances, one has to go forward with some patience. Linguistic theory has not yet reached the world and in my opinion will never do. It will typically be the application of linguistics, rather than linguistics itself, that should build the bridge. Computational linguistics is application oriented only.

Some attention should be paid to the question of the several levels of linguistic meaning and to the way these are accounted for by SELANCA representations. I refer to Jackendoff [1972], who distinguishes: 1) functional meaning, i.e. the relations in the sentence that are induced by the verbs; this level of meaning mainly is the central topic of Fillmore [1968]; 2) modal meaning, i.e. the conditions under which a sentence purports to correspond to situations in the real world; 3) coreferential relations; 4) focus and presupposition. The first of these, the functional meaning, is claimed to be represented fully by the SELANCA expressions. The modal meaning , as Jackendoff uses this term, is unaccounted for, since it is considered to be of importance mainly for the semantic interpretation of the NC, a subject which has not received much attention as yet within our research. Although we implemented in CASUS at a certain moment a theory about coreferency[22], we afterwards decided to renounce this idea, since we considered it unacceptable to indicate negative relations, as are defined by a *non*-coreference rule. It seems correct to consider a set of non-coreference rules as a grammatical constraint on pragmatic interpretation of a sentence. That is a reason to situate these rules somewhere behind the point where the aims of CASUS end, where a choice has to be made between the different semantic interpretations of a sentence, where the context and the situation has to be regarded and other considerations of not purely linguistic nature will ask attention. Since a disambiguation can only be performed totally with the help of information of pragmatic nature, we decided not to try to account for it within the borders of SELANCA. Focus and presupposition are not considered to be part of linguistic meaning as it is conceived of in the present study. I will return to the subject in section 3.2.1.10.

In concluding I make some summarizing remarks. Since language is to be considered as an interpretation of reality, reality as such is unavailable. The only way reality is available to a human being is by being retrieved by his information retrieving system (his organs of sense and his brain) and in second instance by being transmitted by language to other people. Because language is the way reality is available for humans, it will be impossible to loosen meaning from language forms and, by consequence, from words. That is the reason to reject Jackendoff's view that it is clearly desirable *to represent the claims made by a sentence in a canonical form that is independent of the particular lexical items used*. It has to be agreed upon that a semantic theory has to be developed that brings forth the possibility to represent the meaning of a sentence in such a way that all linguistically relevant aspects of it are expressed. My claims about SELANCA hold that this language meets all requirements. I think that SELANCA recedes far enough and at the same time not too far from Dutch. The case theory it reflects may be considered universal, as may be deduced from linguistic discussions in general.

For the time being we do not try to interpret structures with an N or an A as semantic centre because the implementation of the semantic theory about A and N constructions is not yet elaborated that far. A theory about these constructions is only rudimentarily present.

## 3.2 THE TRANSLATION FROM AMAZON TO SELANCA

### 3.2.1 THE LINGUISTIC THEORY

In the next sections we will try to give a detailed account of the way the syntactic structure assigned to a sentence by AMAZON is translated into a SELANCA semantic expression by CASUS. In this section I deal with the overall structure of the algorithm, the main function of which is shown in (1):

(1)

```
Translater
      Load Lexicon
      Redundancies

Read Sentence
      Consult Lexicon
      Pop lexical Information
      Set Main Features
      Detopicalize Reset Verb
      Administrate Satellites

      Interpret Sentence

                 → Read Sentence
```

The function 'Translater' is central in CASUS. As the figure shows, it's first task is the loading of the lexicon. A separate function deals with adding the redundant lexical features to the lexical items. Afterwards an iterative process is started which concerns one sentence at a time. It's starting point is 'Read sentence' in (1). The first part of the process is the consultation of the lexicon, by which function correct associations are made between the words of the sentence and certain lexical items. Note that, until this moment, the words of the sentence lack morphological and semantic feature information. The information structure is merely what is pictured in the tree diagrams. After connecting the lexical items to the words of the sentence, that information is much richer. In order to make semantic information about the sentence's constituents available at their top nodes, the socalled popping of the lexical information takes place, which results in linking e.g. the information stored at an N node on the corresponding NC node (cfr. section 3.2.2.5). The process of setting the main features of the sentence regards the main sentence form that will be lost afterwards: a sentence with an interrogative form is marked as

'QUESTION'. After detopicalization and resetting of the main finite verb (details of which processes will be dealt with in 3.2.1.1 and 3.2.1.2), an array of pointers is built, pointing to the main verbs in the sentence, whose environments will have to be interpreted semantically. This is done by means of the function 'Find Nodes'. The subroutine 'Administrate Satellites' (see nr. 3 in section 2 of the appendix), gathers information about the place in the tree structure where the case candidates for all main verbs are to be found. A subfunction of 'Administrate Satellites' performs reconstruction of verb separation, e.g. *legde ... neer* is changed into *neerlegde* (see section 3.2.1.4). After all this preparatory work has been done, the semantic interpretation strictly speaking takes place. A run of CASUS is terminated when no more sentences may be read. Details of the subroutines mentioned in (1), apart from the function 'Interpret Sentence' and 'Detopicalize and Reset Verb', will only be touched upon incidentally below.

(2) Wie denk jij dat ik probeerde te fotograferen?
(Who think you that I tried to photograph?)

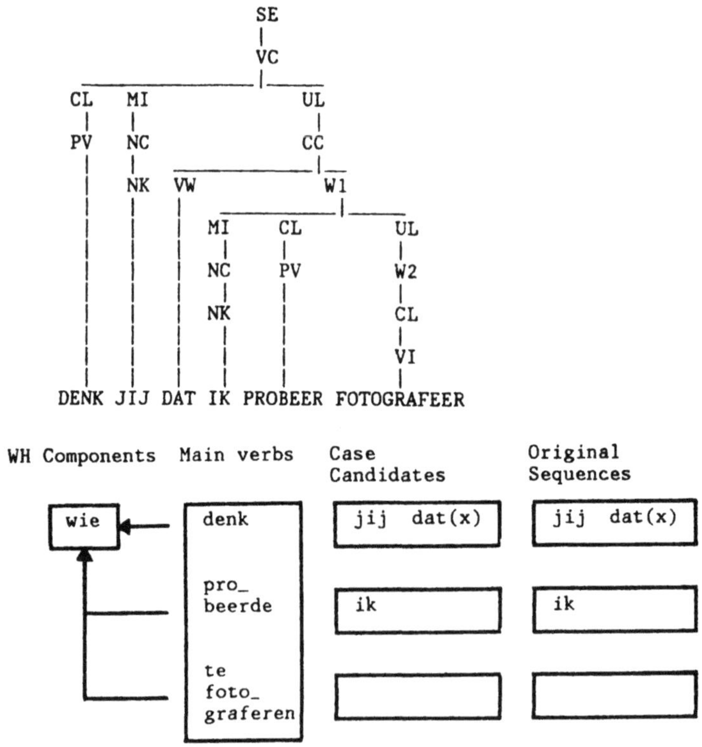


Let us look for a moment to the structure of the information that is built with respect to one sentence when the subroutine 'Administrate Satellites' has done it's job. I illustrate the situation by the figure (2), where the tree structure is shown as well, changed in details, according to what will be dealt with in the next sections. Note by the way, that the WH-constituent *Wie* is not longer present in the tree structure; it has received a special status, since it is to be considered as a possible case candidate for several syntactic levels. Apart from that, mainly a set of ordered (sets of) pointers has been created by means of which it is possible to refer to parts and sets of parts of the sentence. The array F contains pointers to the main verbs, F<1> to the first verb, F<2> to the second verb, and so on. The verbs are collected, processing the tree from left to right and giving preference to depth. Associated with the index of a certain main verb, three arrays have been created: Case candidates<i>, Original Sequence<i> and Trans Node<i>. These arrays contain pointers to the sentence constituents which have to be considered as candidates for semantic functions in connection with the related main verb. Finally, there is the array WH-Component, which contains pointers to the different WH-Constituents or topicalized constituents, which have been detected in the surface environment of certain verbs. Their indexes in the array are to be associated with the indexes of the verbs in array F. We will return to these matters in the next sections. In this section, I will now pay some attention to the 'Interpretation' of the sentence, details of which are indicated in (3). In

(3)

```
1 Next Main Verb
       Expand Case Frames

    2 Next CaseFrame

        3 Next Sequence
               Reset Original Sequence
               Allign WH_component
               Connect Trans Nodes
               Depassivize
               Set Index Sequences
               Change Sequence Casus
               Insert PRO

               Applicable Structure

               Interpret PRO
```

that figure three levels are suggested in connection with which some important subroutines are mentioned. The program iterates on every level, the highest iteration priority being the most imbedded third level, with the indication 'Next Sequence'. In connection with each main verb of a sentence successively, the different case frames are tested and in connection with every case frame the several sequences are considered which have to be hypothesized. Let me explain this globally with reference to several sections below, where things will be dealt with in more detail.

CASUS performs the semantic interpretation of a sentence by performing interpretations of the different semantic kernels (see (9) in 3.1 above) of the sentence. The algorithm has to iterate over the different main verbs. A main verb may be marked lexically by different case frames, so that for a certain main verb there has to be an iteration over different case frames. On the deepest level there has to be another iteration, viz. over the different reconstructions of the sequence the case candidates show in the syntactic surface structure. As will be shown in 3.2.1.8, a case candidate may have been topicalized from different basic positions, e.g. an agentive or a dative position. This implies an ambiguity to which attention has to be paid by hypothesizing different basic positions and consequently iterating over different basic sequences.

In figure (3), a number of crucial subroutines are mentioned on the different levels of iteration. Let me give some brief comments on those here, also with reference to different places below where things will get more detailed discussion. What exactly is the sense of the subroutine 'Expand Case Frames', called from the main iteration level, may better be dealt with in connection with WH-movement (3.2.1.5). At this place I will confine myself to remarking that the expanding of the case frames is a means to control the iteration over the different hypotheses to be tested in connection with the question as to whether the WH-constituent is or is not to be considered as a possible case candidate on a certain level.

The iteration over different case frames implies nothing but choosing the next frame to be tested. The third iteration contains a number of tasks. First, there is the resetting of the original sequence of the case candidates. By a previous test, the sequence of the case candidates may have been changed in connection with a certain hypothesis about the place where a moved constituent was generated originally, and therefore the original order has to be restored. Then, the alligning of the WH-constituent is performed: it is added to the set of case candidates if the hypothesis is to be tested that it has a semantic function in connection with the verb and the case frame at hand. Then follows the connection of the socalled Trans Nodes to the set of case candidates. This operation has to do with the restructuring of raising of sentence constituents; the question will be looked at in section 3.2.1.9 about the S complements. Further, the depassivization of a passive construction takes place. It will be explained in 3.2.1.3 why this has to be done at this level of semantic interpretation. The function 'Set Index Sequences' establishes, which next hypothesis about the original sequence of the candidates has to be considered and, at last, 'Change Sequence Casus' brings the case candidates in the actual order required. The insertation and interpretation of a PRO, just before and after the call of 'Applicable structure' has to do with special syntactic features of S-complements. I refer to section 3.2.1.9 for that subject. The function 'Applicable structure' which is tested next, tests the hypothesis that, with respect to 'this' verb and 'this' case frame and 'this' hypothesis about the original place of the WH-constituent and with 'this' hypothesis about the original sequence of the case candidates, these case candidates as a set meet the claims for subcategorization. The word 'structure' stands for 'case frame' here.

There are some other remarks to be made about the way CASUS performs the semantic interpretation of the sentence, although the very heart of the process seems to be adequately indicated in the foregoing lines. First there is the decision about one total semantic interpretation for a whole sentence. Such interpretation is a certain set of interpretations, found for the different semantic kernels of the sentence. The iteration illustrated in (3) is ended as soon as no other such set can be found. It is clear that a semantic interpretation for the whole sentence has to imply semantic interpretations for all the main verbs of the sentence. As soon as a set of *n* interpretations for the *n* semantic kernels of the sentence is collected, this set will be a semantic interpretation for the sentence if every WH-constituent has received a function in connection with one and not more than one verb. If so, the subroutine 'Write result' writes a copy of the tree structure of the sentence, in the form it has recieved by what may be called semantic transformations, to an output dataset.

Still some other things regarding the interpretation process have to be mentioned in this introducing section. I will dwell for a moment upon a not unimportant aspect of the interpreting algorithm. As may be clear already, the SELANCA expressions are obtained by changing the sentence structure. Constituents which play a semantic role in connection with a certain main verb of the sentence are detached from their original places and attached to the node of that verb as it's sons. In that way the structure of the sentence is changed continuously while the semantic interpretation is taking place. It often happens that, after a certain interpretation regarding a certain main verb has been applied, the algorithm returns to that same verb and tries another interpretation that may very well succeed. In that case the algorithm would have to operate on an already changed tree structure, thus requiring a defining of the interpreting process for both changed and unchanged tree structures. To avoid this necessity, the administration is organized in such a way that it does not matter where the case candidates, pointed at at some moment, actually reside. Thus, the only way the sentence tree has to be corrected in order to yield an acceptable situation for a semantic transformation to take place, is clearing the set of pointers from a verb to it's sons. After that the case candidates are given their functions, according to the claims of a second or third case frame, and they are attached to the verb. It will be clear that the organization of the interpreting work under CASUS consists of defining a great number of subroutines (functions) which operate on one globally available tree structure representation. Certain computer programs define a situation where the data is wandering through a wood of functions, other show a situation where the functions, like an army of agricultural machinery, are ploughing and farming a continuously changing field. To my imagination CASUS is an instance of the latter.

In the description and demonstration of the way CASUS performs the semantic interpretation, given in the following sections, we will use certain sentences, such as, for instance;

(4) Wie dacht Karel dat het gedaan had?
(Who thought Charles that it done had)

Of course, the example sentences used will have to be in Dutch. It will be useful, however, to add translations, which will be given in correct English or, like is done in (4), in a word to word transliteration, which gives an idea about the meaning and, at the same time, about Dutch syntax. It will not be indicated which of both is actually meant, neither will the choice of translation or transliteration be motivated.

The analysis will be illustrated by showing the sentence structure in it's different states. It should be noticed that all tree images appearing in the exposition are generated by CASUS itself. In that way, they are proofs of the algorithm working correctly. Our demonstration will sometimes, for the sake of linguistic coherence, leave for a moment the sequence of things happening in CASUS. Mainly however, we will follow the algorithm step by step. This way of dealing with things will illustrate in what degree theoretical and algorithmic questions interfere. It is our conviction that this interference itself is of significant importance for all applications of linguistic theories.

### 3.2.1.1 DETOPICALIZATION

Sentence (1) is analyzed by AMAZON as is shown in (2):

(1) Wie dacht Karel dat het gedaan had?

(2)

```
                          SE
 _________________________|_
 NC                        VC
 |      ___________________|_______
 NK     PV      MI                UL
 |      |       |                 |
 |      |       NC                CC
 |      |       |       __________|_
 |      |       NK     VW          W1
 |      |       |      |     ______|_
 |      |       |      |     MI      CL
 |      |       |      |     |     __|__
 |      |       |      |     NC   VD     14
 |      |       |      |     |    |      |
 |      |       |      |     NK   |      |
 |      |       |      |     |    |      |
WIE   DACHT   KAREL   DAT   HET  GEDAAN  HAD
```

As we discussed in 2.1, the theoretical relevance of an AMAZON interpretation of a sentence's surface structure is the availibility of the constituents subcategorized by a verb on one and the same syntactic level of representation. Apart from WH-movement phenomena, this claim is met in the environment of *gedaan* in (2). In connection with *dacht* however, the subcategorized constituents appear on different levels. *Karel* and *dat het gedaan had* are both nephews, while *wie* is an uncle of *dacht*. It is clear that topicalization is responsible for the fact.

In order to create comparable situations in the environment of all verbs of a sentence, we first change the tree by undoing the topicalization transformation. The transformational operation CASUS uses for that purpose, is performed by the subroutine 'Detopicalize Reset Verb'. The result is shown in (3).

Since it has not yet been subject to any investigation, it is at this moment still unknown to the algorithm that the reconstruction concerns a WH-constituent. The question however is only relevant at the moment a case frame of *denken* is tested. Until then it is sufficient to administrate the original status of the first constituent under MI. An interrogative sentence consists of a VC only. Therefore, after the detopicalization, a sentence marked as a question cannot have a constituent under MI that was originally topicalized. The first constituent under MI of a sentence that was not marked as a QUESTION has to be considered always as an originally topicalized part. (We will return to that subject in 3.2.1.10). That is why the marking of questionary sentences is performed before the detopicalization takes place. For the detopicalizing subroutine the resulting information about the interrogative form is in turn a reason to return without further activity.

(3)

```
                       SE
                       |
                       VC
       ________________|________
CL            MI               UL
|           __|__               |
PV      NC       NC             CC
|       |        |        ______|_
|       NK       NK    VW         W1
|       |        |     |       ___|__
|       |        |     |     MI      CL
|       |        |     |     |     __|__
|       |        |     |     NC   VD    14
|       |        |     |     |    |     |
|       |        |     |     NK   |     |
|       |        |     |     |    |     |
DENK   WIE     KAREL  DAT   HET  DOE   HEB
```

The destination of the original first sentence constituent is the MI-node under VC. According to the AMAZON theory, a VC node is always present. A VC node, however, may lack a MI node, in which case the replacing can only be performed after adding such a node.

After detopicalization, the sentence structure does not show any more differences between different verbal structures on different syntactic levels of representation. The collection of candidates in the different environments can thus be performed in the same way on all levels.

### 3.2.1.2 RESETTING OF V

A canonic transformational grammar of a language like Dutch contains a rule which predicts the correct place of a finite verb in a sentence like (1):

(1)

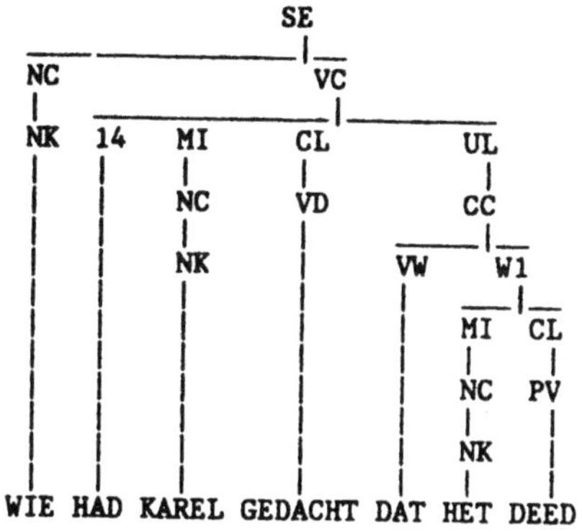


The hypothesis that Dutch is an SOV language has to imply a transfomational rule which brings the finite verb to it's initial position, separated occasionally from another verbal form in the end of the construction. It is a well-known fact that this transformation operates only in main clauses. Subclauses show the finite verb on it's original place:

(2) ... dat Karel gedacht *had* dat ik meeging

(3)

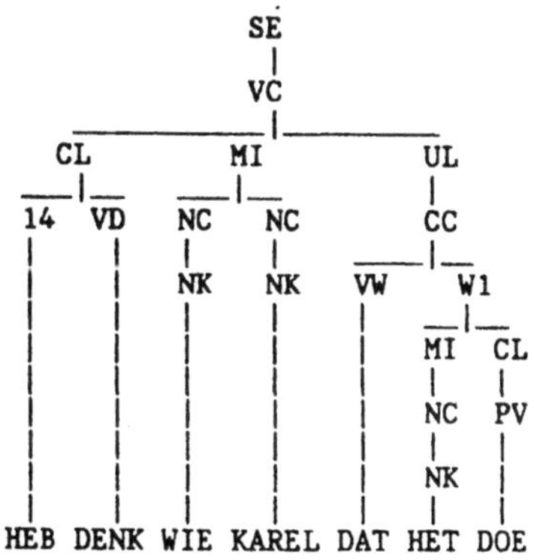


The transformation that places the finite verb in initial position under VP is called V-setting. For the same reason as we performed the socalled detopicalization (see 3.2.1.1) we also implemented a reversion of the V-setting transformation. After the finite verb in main clauses has been reset to it's original place, there will be no difference left between main and subclauses in this respect.

The resetting is performed in the same subroutine which also takes care of the detopicalization. The main clause construction is inspected to see whether there is a CL (verbal cluster) node. In a sentence like (1) there is. In such a case, the finite verb is attached to this CL node as it's first son. In cases where there is no such node, a new one is first added and the finite verb is attached to it as it's only son. The construction (3) is the result for sentence (1).

### 3.2.1.3 DEPASSIVIZATION

Since, in our opinion, the verb is the meaning center of the sentence, all effort is done to warrant a consistent way of analyzing it's environment. We try to use an interpreting algorithm which has no other concern than to assign semantic functions to constituents, regardless of their sequence or any other unessential feature of the actual structure. This was also the background of the detopicalization and resetting of the verb. In very much the same way it is the motivation of the depassivization of passive constructions.

There is more than one theory which accounts for the meaning relation between a passive construction and it's active counterpart. The SELANCA structures require the collection of the constituents that play a semantic role in relation to a certain verb, so a transformational reconstruction is implicitly required. Every node which has been displaced for some reason has to be brought back to it's original place before the semantic role assignment can be performed. In relation with this it is evidently preferable to reconstruct passive constructions transformationally. CASUS performs changes in passive constructions by which the case assigning subroutine need not worry about an agentive, appearing as a PC, or an objective, functioning as a grammatical subject.

For a restructuring algorithm, a number of questions have to be answered and a number of problems have to be solved. The first question is at what moment the depassivization has to be started. In a sentence like (1)

(1) Door wie zei Jan dat de opmerking gemaakt was?
    (By whom told John that the comment made was)

the WH-constituent *Door wie* will be considered as a possible case candidate for a semantic function in relation with *gemaakt*. (For details with respect to WH-movement see 3.2.1.5). Let us suppose that one configuration of candidates around *gemaakt* has already been tested and that the test failed. Then the WH-constituent will have to be lined up with the candidates at the level of that verb and the test will have to be repeated. If the construction was in passive voice, the depassivization must be repeated also, since the adding of a new constituent may alter the situation significantly. If the configuration of constituents should still be the same as during the previous test, the depassivization need not be repeated. Generally speaking the depassivization has to take place when the first test of a case frame is going to start start and, if the same case frame is to be tested, when the configuration of the candidates has changed by adding a new constituent.

The inspection of the situation implies first an investigation of the auxiliary verbs that are gathered on the variable ASPECT of the main verb considered. (See for data structure details 3.2.2.3). A passive construction necessarily contains the auxiliary *zijn* or *worden*. When the auxiliary *zijn* is met, a more detailed inspection of the main verb's lexical features is needed for a correct conclusion about passivity. Look for that sake at sentences like:

(2) Hij is zijn vader opgevolgd.
(He is his father succeeded)
Hij is door zijn zoon opgevolgd.
(He is by his son succeeded)

The first sentence is in active, the second in passive voice. According to the analysis of Klieverik [1983], the algorithm tests whether the verb is lexically marked as claiming two of the following cases: agentive, dative, objective and factitive. If the test fails, the sentence will not be considered to be in passive voice. Even when the case frame of *opvolgen* (succeed) claims both an agentive and an objective, it will not be possible to attain the correct conclusions with respect to the first sentence of (2). Extra information is needed about the mutative or immutative meaning of the verb.

The function 'Depassivize' causes a structural change in the passive construction. The change concerns the following details. If the construction lacks a PC with the preposition *door* (by), a dummy constituent will be created and marked for those features that are demanded in the lexicon for the main verb in question. If there happens to be such a PC, CASUS will look whether it is marked for these features and, if so, change the PC into a corresponding NC. The dummy constituent in the first instance and this NC, transformed out of PC in the second instance, is put on the first place in the data object that contains the case candidates for the verb. The intention is to warrant that also the place is adequate for the case assigning algorithm that has to operate later on. See 3.2.1.8 for questions of order of the case candidates.

As will be shown in 3.2.1.10 (about ambiguity and semantic equivalence) and 3.2.1.8, CASUS is capable to detect the two possible readings for e.g.

(3) Jan gaf Piet een boek.
(John gave Peter a book.)

Both *Jan* and *Piet* may be interpreted as agentive and as dative. This ability can easily become a disability for the sentence

(4) Door Jan werd Piet een boek gegeven.
(By John was Peter a book given)

when it has been changed by 'Depassivize' into

(5)

```
                      SE
                      |
                      VC
             _________|_________
            CL                  MI
       _____|____         ______|_____
      |          VD      NC    NC     NC
      |        __|__     |     |    __|__
      |       |     MO   NK    NK  LW    NK
      |       |     |    |     |   |     |
      |       |     14   |     |   |     |
      |       |     |    |     |   |     |
   PASSIEF  GEEF  WORD  JAN  PIET EEN  BOEK
```

In this situation, the original passive voice is a decisive detail that may not be neglected. The verbal construction is therefore explicitly marked as 'Passive' in order to prevent unwanted side effects. See for details schema (7) of section 3.2.1.8 with discussion.

The case assigning algorithm may now start. However, some aspects of the passive problem still play a role. The test for the semantic functions agentive (sometimes dative) has to imply controling the socalled agreement with the main verb (or with one of it's auxiliaries). In originally passive constructions, the test has to be performed with respect to the object, because that part is the original grammatical subject. Put the other way round: to a constituent in an originally passive construction, the role of objective may only be assigned, if it obeys agreement. With respect to the agentive, the test has to be omitted in that environment.

An example semantic interpretation of the passive sentence

(6) Zij werd aangesteld tot burgemeester.
(She was appointed as a mayor)

is shown in (7). The reader is referred to section 3.2.1.7 for the semantic interpretation of the attribute and it's object.

By the explanation of section 3.2.1 it has become clear, that the depassivization is included in the deepest iteration level of the subroutine 'Interpret Sentence'; see figure (3) of that section. One may wonder why the algorithm has been built like that. Since a certain semantic interpretation may entail,

(7)

```
                              SE
         ----------------------|---
         |                          VD
         |        -----------------|-----------
         |        |      MO  NC AGE            PC ATT
         |        |      |    |          ---------|--
         |        |      14   NK    VZ              NC
         |        |      |    |     |          ----|--------
         |        |      |    |     |          |          NC OBJ
         |        |      |    |     |          |             |
PASSIEF AANSTEL WORD  XDUM  TOT BURGEMEESTER   ZIJ
```

that an attribute (see section 3.2.1.7) is attached to some case candidate, a resetting of the original sequence of the case candidates has to be performed after every interpretation. But, since a resetting implies an undoing of a previous depassivization, the depassivization will have to be repeated after a resetting. The depassivization will therefore have to be performed every time a new sequence of the case candidates is considered. I may add, that in order to correctly perform the depassivization, also the WH-constituent will have to be alligned again, since it may be a critical element, e.g. a PC with preposition *door*.

The depassivization as part of CASUS was first reported in Klieverik [1983] and Van Bakel [1983a].

### 3.2.1.4 SEPARATED PARTS OF VERBS

Dutch syntax shows a typical difference with for instance English with respect to the way the socalled separable verbs are treated. See (1):

(1) He put his pencil down.
When he put his pencil down.
Hij legde zijn potlood neer.
Toen hij zijn potlood neerlegde.

It seems a problem what is the nature of the adverbial element. Is it a part of a verb, just like the element *under* in the verb *to undergo*, or is it an adverb as it seems to be in the English sentences of (1)? More relevant than this question is the fact that the particle should be handled in the same way in the combination *legde neer* as in *neerlegde*. Both forms have to be associated with one lexical item or, for that matter, with the same pair of lexical items. Because we did not want to split up one "word" into two different ones, we decided, according to traditional grammatical ideas, to treat them as separated parts of a verb. The implication was, that we had to reconstruct a form *neerlegde* on the basis of *legde neer*.

As is mentioned above, the syntax of AMAZON defines a lexical category AV, the adverbial particle. (See production rule 9 in section 1 of the Appendix). To the adverbial parts of separated verb forms this category is assigned by AMAZON's morphological analyzer. When both parts of the verb are not separated in a sentence, the morphological analyzer assigns to both parts together the category that would have been assigned to the verbal part alone. *legde neer* appears as VSUBPO(legde) AVO(neer), *neerlegde* as VSUBPO(neerlegde) in the input for AMAZON's syntax.

Before CASUS starts the semantic interpretation at the level of a verbal construction, a subroutine is started ('Allign AV'; see section 2 of the Appendix) which looks for an occurrence of an AV in that environment. If an AV is met, the node is deleted and it's lexical element is connected with the main verb. This will be done in such a way that a form is yielded that has a representation in the lexicon, viz. as one of the variants (see 3.2.2.2) of the complex verb concerned. After this operation has been performed, the connection with the lexicon will be reestablished, so there will be no longer a pointing to the item *leggen* but to *neerleggen*. In (2) the sentence state is shown as it results from syntactic analysis:

(2)

```
                        SE
       _________________|_
      NC                 VC
      |        __________|__
      NK   PV               MI
      |    |             ___|_______
      |    |             NC        AV
      |    |        _____|_        |
      |    |        LW      NK     |
      |    |        |       |      |
     HIJ LEGDE ZIJN POTLOOD NEER
```

(3) Shows the form after detopicalization:

(3)

```
                     SE
                     |
                     VC
       ______________|_
      CL               MI
      |      __________|__________
      PV   NC          NC        AV
      |    |        ___|_        |
      |    NK   LW       NK      |
      |    |    |        |       |
     LEG HIJ ZIJN POTLOOD NEER
```

In (4) the form is shown after the alligning of AV has taken place:

(4)

```
                    SE
                    |
                    VC
       _____________|___
      CL                MI
      |        _________|_
      PV      NC          NC
      |       |      _____|_
      |       NK   LW       NK
      |       |    |        |
   NEERLEG HIJ ZIJN POTLOOD
```

The way the AV is treated under CASUS was reported earlier in Huiskens and Wever [1983].

### 3.2.1.5 WH-MOVEMENT

A well-known feature of natural languages is the socalled WH-movement: a constituent with specific features is moved to the COMP position of the S where it is generated and, according to the character of the verb at the next higher level, to the COMP position of that higher S, and so on, until the COMP of the highest S is reached. As soon as the raised constituent meets an S structure without a verb with the features needed for the move to continue correctly, or when more than one binding node should be crossed, the move cannot be performed. See he sentences (1), the first of which shows the WH-movement up to the highest COMP and the second a movement that is restricted to a lower level:

(1) Wie dacht Jan dat ik zei dat ik probeerde te fotograferen?
(Who thought John that I told that I tried to photograph?)
Hier is nu de man die mij vertelde wie (dat) hij probeerde te fotograferen.
(Here is now the man who me told who he tried to photograph).

If the moved constituent is left in the COMP of an embedded S, there is a possibility in substandard Dutch to use the conjunction *dat* on that level too, as is indicated in the second example sentence. Both types of movement are grammatical, when +WH constituents are concerned. However, there is a similar movement in Dutch syntax of −WH constituents. Look at the sentences of (2):

(2) Jan dacht hij dat ik zei dat ik probeerde te fotograferen.
* Hier is nu de man die mij vertelde Jan (dat) hij probeerde te fotograferen.

Questions about the syntactic differences between the types of (1) and (2) are dealt with in some detail by Scholten, Evers and Klein [1981]. The main difference is that a −WH constituent has to land at the highest COMP position in order for the sentence to be grammatical, while a +WH constituent may be left at any intermediate level.

According to general convention, I will refer to the first movement type with the term WH-movement and to the second one with topicalization. In this section I deal with both transformations at the same time, because of the important similarities between them and also because, for that reason, CASUS handles them by means of the same functions. This is possible since CASUS need not account for the ungrammaticalness of the second sentence of (2), which is discarded by AMAZON(83) already: a subclause of the form *NC NC probeerde te fotograferen*, not following a subordination conjunction, is ungrammatical anyway if it's first NC is characterized −WH.

WH-movement and topicalization are controlled by two operations. The first is performed within the subroutine 'Administrate satellites' (see section 3.2.1 sub (1)), the second, called 'Allign WH-Component', is repeated, within the second level iteration of Interpret sentence, for every sequence of the case candidates (see section 3.2.1 sub (3)). Let us first look at the part of the processing that precedes the semantic interpretation of the separate main verbs, I mean the part in 'Administrate satellites'. Before the semantic interpretation starts, the following investigations are performed for every main verb of the sentence. First, a pointer is set to the WH-constituent on top of the bridge, in order to indicate that that constituent has to be considered as a possible case candidate in relation to the verb of this syntactic level. For a correct conclusion, the structure of the bridge has to be analysed in order to find the constituent. A bridge along which WH-movement and topicalization can take place has to meet the following claims: the bridge consists of a number of syntactic levels, each of which contains a socalled bridge verb together with an embedded S, +tense or −tense, and, in the former case, having the conjunction *dat*:

(3) ... V (bridge verb) ... (S *dat* ...
... V (bridge verb) ... (S ... *te* Inf ...

In case of possible topicalization, the highest level of the bridge has to be the sentence level; in case of WH-movement this highest level may be found on every sentence level. If the verb tested appears within an S construction of (3), it need not be itself a bridge verb; a bridge verb typically deepens the bridge or, seen from below, admits a constituent, moved locally to a complementizer position, to ascend to it's own syntactic level. If the claims are met for a certain verb, a pointer is set from 'this' verb to the constituent which, at the higher level, has been marked as a possibly raised element, which consequently has to be regarded as a case candidate for one of the other verbs of the bridge or for the bottom verb under the lowest bridge level:

(4) NC ... V ... (S ... V ...(S ... t ... Vx ))

In (4) V means 'bridge verb', Vx 'no matter what kind of verb', NC is the raised constituent and *t* it's trace. Note, that placing the trace is deciding where the NC has been generated. From an interpretative point of view, this is actually what has to be aimed at.

This is the first operation concerning WH-movement under 'Administrate Satellites'. It is performed in relation to every separate main verb of the sentence. It should be noticed by the way, that the separation of raised verbs out of their surface environments into separate syntax level clusters has taken place previously, so that indeed all different syntax levels are regarded. See for this matter section 3.2.1.9 on the interpretation of S complements. It should be noticed also, that, since the investigation will be repeated in connection with every verb separately, the inspection of the validity of the bridge need not be expanded more than one syntax level at the time. The pointer to the WH-constituent on top of a bridge will automatically expand itself as widely as is needed.

This is a good point to connect on for some remarks about a second operation under 'Administrate Satellites' as regards the WH-movement. If the verb of a certain syntax level has the features of a bridge verb (and will consequently have an S complement, if the sentence is grammatical), the first sentence part that is a case candidate will possibly have been generated on a deeper level. This will be true for no matter what kind of constituent if the highest level of the sentence is concerned, and for a +WH constituent on deeper levels. If the first constituent meets these claims, a pointer is set from this level's verb to that constituent. This pointer will be copied for deeper levels according to what was explained instantly under point one.

The setting of a pointer from a certain verb to the WH-constituent or topicalized constituent on the level where that constituent is found in surface structure (the second operation) takes place after the setting of a pointer to the WH-constituent or topicalized constituent of the next higher level (the first operation). This means, that the second setting may overrule the first one. This is in accord with the rule which says that a syntactic bridge is broken up by a COMP position that is already filled and just this is the case if, on a deeper level, a +WH constituent is met. Look at the following example:

(5) * Wie dacht Jan dat ik zei dat wie probeerde te fotograferen?
(Who thought John that I told that who tried to photograph?)

By the first operation, a pointer is set on the WH variable (see section 3.2.2.3 for this detail) of *probeerde* to the constituent pointed at by *zei*, namely the constituent, pointed at by *dacht*, i.e. (the first) *Wie*. By the second operation afterwards, this pointer is overwritten by a pointer to (the second) *wie*, being this a +WH constituent in the complementizer position of this verb. Since in that way the first *Wie* will get no adequate place, the sentence will get no Selanca representation and is discarded per definition.

I have to speak now about the way the WH-constituents are treated during the semantic interpretation strictly speaking, viz. the operations indicated in (3) of section 3.2.1. In that figure the subroutine 'Allign WH-Component' was mentioned. Let us see what it does exactly. The result of the investigations dealt with so far is that, with respect to all verbs of the sentence, it has become clear in principle which constituents may function as semantic roles in connection with them. When it is not to be excluded that a WH-constituent has possibly been generated on more than one other level, the sentence will be ambiguous, perhaps even more than twice. Look at the sentence (6):

(6) Morgen zegt Jan dat hij denkt dat Anja verliefd wordt.
(Tomorrow says John that he thinks that Anja falls in love)

which is three times ambiguous, since every level of the sentence is the possible origin of *Morgen*. This means that the moved constituent *morgen* will have to be hypothesized to have been generated on every sentence level separately. An acceptable semantic interpretation of the sentence will be every set of interpretations of all semantic kernels in which *morgen* will appear exactly once, no matter in connection with which verb, if for every semantic kernel the set of lexical claims is met. The algorithm has to decide whether or not in connection with a certain verb the hypothesis that the moved constituent was generated at 'this' level has to be tested. It is clear, that the hypothesis may be skipped if the constituent was already assigned a semantic function on a higher level. This is exactly what the function 'Allign WH-Component' does. If the relevant WH-constituent is still free, the hypothesis is considered and, if met, the semantic function is assigned to the constituent. It is clear, that it is impossible to assign a semantic function to a WH-constituent twice. Since it is not excluded, however, that in connection with no verb of the sentence it has been taken into account, a specific inspection about this has to be performed when the last verb of the sentence has been treated.

In figure (3) of section 3.2.1 the subroutine 'Expand features' was mentioned, which has an administrative task as regards the WH-movement. As a means to control the iteration that is needed for treating adequately the hypotheses about the place where the WH-constituent was generated, that subroutine generates the information that every separate case frame of a verb has to be considered once with and once without the assumption that the WH-constituent originates from 'this' level. This is done by simply copying every frame and marking the copies as +WH. The way that information is used is shown in section 4 of the Appendix.

### 3.2.1.6 SEMANTIC DUMMIES

The semantic interpretation that is performed by CASUS is mainly a process of testing a set of constituents to see whether it meets as a whole the set of claims that are defined for a certain verb in the lexicon. If the sentence seems to be not a maximal projection of the lexical frame of the verb, the interpreter has to discard it. In certain well-defined situations, however, a sentence may go in order, although the claims are not met. We have to distinguish the situation that not to all of the semantic functions claimed individually a constituent can be assigned and, on the opposite, that a constituent is left without having been assigned to a semantic function. In the former case, rules will have to apply to attract constituents from elsewhere. Such situations are accounted for by WH-movement and raising. The latter case is dealt with in this section. It is characterized by the fact that for one semantic function more than one sentence constituent is available. We will claim that one of these is a dummy constituent, which only functions as a reference to the other, which bears the relevant semantic information and is the real semantic argument claimed by the verb. Look at the following sentences:

(1) Het valt mee dat hij dat weet.
(It is a windfall that he knows it)
Ik reken erop dat je komt.
(I count on your coming)

In the first example the pronoun *Het* is, so to say, a pointer to the constituent *dat hij dat weet* and in the same way *erop* in the second example to *dat je komt*. These dummy constituents are to be accounted for by merely syntactic rules, i.e. rules which do not claim a semantic representation within our framework. This means, that the following sentences have the same meaning:

(2) Het valt mee dat hij dat weet.
Dat hij dat weet valt mee.

Even if an occasional topicalization would be claimed to have a specific meaning feature that ought to be accounted for explicitly, also within the current framework, the constituent *het* would still have to be considered as a dummy without any semantic function and the first sentence of (2) as a sentence without topicalized constituent. The difference between the sentences (2) is merely that topicalization has taken place in the second instance. Note, that the situation in the second sentence in (1) is different in this respect that there cannot be built a pair like (3):

(3) Ik reken erop dat je komt.
 * Dat je komt reken ik op[23].

Because the syntax of Dutch does not allow preposition stranding, this sentence does not allow topicalization. Notice, however, that the topicalization is not of principal importance for the facts observed, as is shown by:

(4) Mij valt het mee dat hij het weet.
 (To me it seems a stroke of luck that he knows it.)

In this sentence also a dummy pronoun *het* is observed, the function of which is merely syntactic, so that constituent need not be accounted for semantically within our framework. The same holds for *erop* in the example (3)[24].

If the pronominal dummy is only of syntactic relevance, functioning only for internal organization of syntactic structure, it has to be deleted by the semantic interpreter. The interpreter, however, should first detect which sentence parts have to be considered as semantic dummies. If it is an adverbial pronoun like *erop*, *ernaar*, merely deleting the constituent would not be adequate, since not only a pointer would be lost (which would do no harm), but also it's typical form, namely it's second part, bearing information about the preposition that governs the object of the verb concerned. A verb like *verlangen* (to long for) should be defined lexically as claiming an object in the form of a prepositional phrase with *naar*:

(5) Zij verlangde naar haar kinderen
 (She was longing for her children)
 Zij verlangde ernaar dat zij haar kinderen terug zou zien
 (She was longing to see her children again)

The lexicon should generalize over the sentences of (5), which means, that in some way the information should be kept, that *ernaar* has to be associated with the preposition *naar*. Therefore the second example sentence should be changed in such a way that a PC appears, starting with the appropriate preposition.

The function 'Delete dummies' starts with an inspection of the case candidates, in order to see whether there is both a conjunction construction starting with *dat* and a dummy constituent in the form of *het* or a pronominal adverb of the form *ermee*, *erin*, *ernaar*, etc. If the dummy is the pronoun *het*, this has only to be deleted. In the other case, the construction is altered, in the way that is shown in the following schemas. Afterwards, the semantic interpretation can be executed without difficulties.

(6)

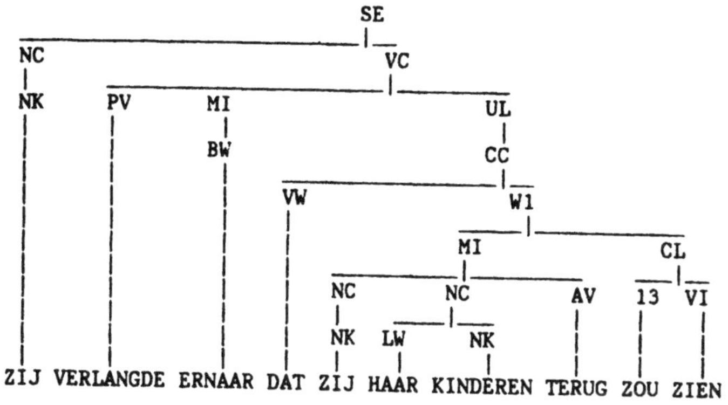


(7)

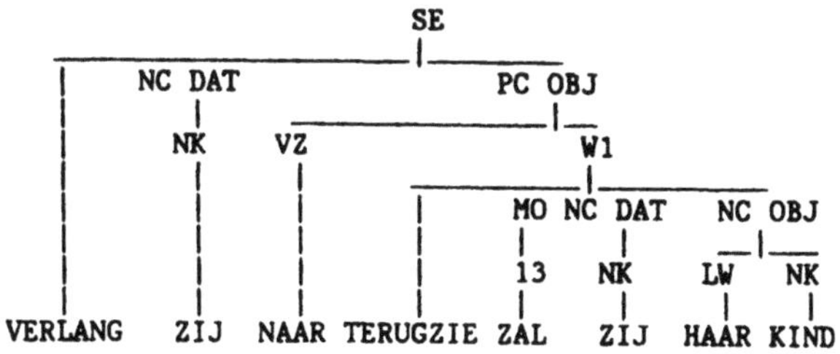


While in (6) the UL consists of a CC (conjunction construction), this constituent has disappeared in (7), where a PC (prepositional construction) has been put in it's place. This PC consists of a preposition *naar* and a subclause (W1), which would mean in terms of surface structure:

(8) naar (zij haar kinderen terug zou zien)

It need hardly be mentioned, that the SELANCA expression should not be judged in connection with surface structure however. For the sentence shown in (6) and (7), the AMAZON structure and the SELANCA expression respectively, the lexical definition used for the verb *verlangen* was:

(9) DAT(),OBJ(/PC/NAAR),*

It should be pointed out, that no effort was made to control other situations with more than one candidate for one case function. Look at the following examples:

(10) Daaraan had hij niet gedacht, dat het kon gaan regenen.
(He had not thought that it could start raining)
Waarom had hij verwacht dat Lucie zou koken?
(Why did he expect that Lucy would cook?)

By comparing these sentences, it will become clear how difficult it would be to conclude to a dummy pronoun in the first but not in the second example. It seems to be impossible to decide beforehand, i.e. before a certain case frame is tested in connection with a set of candidates, whether or not adverbial pronouns like *daaraan*, *waarom* should be considered to be semantic dummies. The function 'Delete dummies' is as yet called by 'Administrate satellites', which is positioned outside the semantic interpretation strictly speaking. This would have to be changed in order to take correct conclusions about sentences like (10). In connection with an apparently simple question as is dealt with in this section, quite some problems have still to be solved. Note by the way that there are instances like (11), with an adverbial pronoun *eraan* in unaccented form, which are too difficult for the algorithm in it's present form:

(11) Hij voegde eraan toe dat hij het jammer vond.

If the deletion of dummies would be situated within the iteration that is characterized by figure (3) of section 3.2.1., everything could work correctly.

### 3.2.1.7 ATTRIBUTES

It need hardly be emphasized that the concept of SELANCA originates in a long-lasting involvement in grammatical analysis and description of Dutch sentences, rather than in theoretical reflections on language and meaning in general. The observation of the properties of certain sentence parts, namely the attributes I am going to deal with in this section, was the basis for extending Fillmore's set of case functions with the function: Attribute. I will have to show that this extension is necessary to account for certain meaning phenomena that are unaccounted for in Fillmore [1968] and to illustrate how the semantic interpretation is performed.

Traditionally, Dutch grammars contain descriptions of what is called *bepalingen van gesteldheid* (adjuncts of state), by which term sentence parts are indicated that describe the state in which another sentence part (or rather it's object referred to) is being 1. during the activity etc. indicated by the sentence's predicate, or 2. according to that activity, or 3. as a result of that activity. See the examples of (1), (2) and (3) respectively:

(1) *Rauw* lust ik die groente niet.
(I do not like those vegetables uncooked)
Men kijkt *lichtelijk geërgerd* op als ...
(One looks up somewhat annoyed when ...)
*Gebakken* heb ik ze liever.
(I like them better fried)
*Zuchtend* ging hij zitten.
(He sat down with a sigh)

(2) Ik vind vis *lekker*.
(I like fish)
Hij beschouwde mij *als de aanstichter*.
(He considered me as the instigator)
Dat noem ik *stom*.
(I call that stupid)

(3) Hij liep zijn voeten *stuk*.
(He walked his feet sore)
Zij streek de plooien *glad*.
(She stroked the pleats flat)
Hij lachte zich *krom*.
(He died with laughter)
Hij werd *tot commissaris* benoemd.
(He was appointed as a director).

These examples represent fairly adequately the different types of attributes, although not all possible forms are indicated[25].

The theoretical environment that looks most suitable for dealing with the subject at hand is created by Williams [1975]; in Chomsky [1981] some attention is paid to the question at several places, without dealing however with attributes as such and surely without discussing the semantics. The reason for Chomsky to speak about the attributes is their problematic state as regards the θ-roles. For all kind of attributes the description claims a generation in a socalled small clause, as we will see an S construction without a verb. We will have to distinguish attributes which are to be considered to play a θ-role in connection with a verb and others which function as predicates in relation with a noun primarily. Let us look at these two possibilities first: 1. the small S-clause is generated with an adjective as it's head and a PRO constituent as a θ-role carrier; the PRO has to be coindexed with some NC outside the small clause; 2. the small S-clause is generated, containing an adjective as it's head and an NC as a θ-role carrier in connection with that adjective; the NC is raised to an NC position of the matrix, leaving a trace in the small clause. The first possibility is observed in sentences of type (1), the second in sentences of the types (2) and (3). See (4):

(4) [PRO Rauw] lust ik die groente niet.
Ik vind vis [ t lekker].
Hij liep zijn voeten [ t stuk].

These hypotheses follow naturally from general features of linguistic theory: a constituent that has no θ-role cannot be generated in the domain of a head otherwise than lexically empty; to every constituent in the domain of a head, a θ-role has to be assigned according to the lexical subcategorization features of the head. The verb *liep* (walked) in the last sentence of (4), which is supposed not to subcategorize an object, may not admit in it's domain the constituent *zijn voeten* (his feet). For that reason we must hypothesize that this constituent has been generated in a small clause, say

(5) (S (NC zijn voeten) (A stuk) )

where the A is to be considered as the head and the NC as some semantic argument in connection with that head. In the same way, the second example sentence of (4) has to be explained. We consider *vind* as an intransitive verb and postulate that the constituent *vis* (fish) has been generated in a small clause with the head *lekker* (delicious). Note that in this analysis a second lexical structure is assumed for the verb *vinden* (to find), apart from another structure for the more common meaning: to find something somewhere. In both sentences raising is supposed to have been at work, yielding structures with the noun phrases appearing in the matrix. The first example of (4), however, is totally different. Here, the NC *die groente* (those vegetables) has to be viewed as an objective in connection with *lust* (to like). Therefore, a small clause has to be hypothesized with a PRO subject, which has to be interpreted semantically by some coindexation.

The surface structures of sentences like (4) have some features in common: they all show an attribute which behaves like a constituent of the matrix: it is a sentence part on it's own, not connected directly with the constituent with which it has some semantic relation, and it even may be topicalized. In all cases, we have to hypothesize a small clause, whose phonetic material behaves as a separate sentence part and e.g. also may be topicalized. For a semantic representation in SELANCA expressions, however, we must build different structures for both types: the NC will have to be connected with it's semantic head and the same holds for the A. It is quite easy to find a solution for the type with raising: we lower the constituent to the small clause with head A and interpret the A as a θ-argument (case function) of the matrix verb, extending in that way Fillmore's case theory.

A little bit more problematic is a semantic representation of the other structure. It would be thinkable to insert a PRO in a small clause, which would have to be introduced as such, and try to state in the SELANCA-expression to build, that this has the same reference as NC so and so. The most weighty argument against this is, that the semantic function of the small clause itself would have to be expressed as well and that no better solution seems to be available than stating, that this also is to be connected with the NC, referred to already by the PRO. This consideration has led to another representation: the small clause as a whole is attached, as a semantic argument in the sense of the language SELANCA, to the semantic kernel N, being the head of the NC which would have to be coindexed with the PRO of the small clause. The PRO vanishes and the semantic relation is expressed by subordination of an ordered pair to the semantic kernel.

The syntactic category of the different small clauses needs some comment. In Chomsky [1981] it is sometimes typified as an S, sometimes as an A. I think it is quite clear that what I call a free attribute, can be viewed as an S. Look at the example (6):

(6) [S [Als financieel-economisch deskundige] [A werkzaam] [bij de directie kunsten van WVC]] vertegenwoordigt hij op het ministerie een invloedrijke stroming, die vindt dat het met de volledig kostendekkende subsidies maar eens afgelopen moet zijn. (HP 8 okt 1983 p.54)

The only difference between the small clause as in (6) and a normal S seems to be the occurrence of an A instead of a V as the head[26]. Small clauses, however, that function as bound attributes are less easily to expand in this way. While in a construction like (6) even high level adverbs (*tot mijn spijt*, *gelukkig* etc.) can be used, there is almost no possibility to expand a bound attribute:

(7) * Als gelukkig burgemeester in Amsterdam werd zij benoemd.
 * Meestal dagelijks lekker vind ik vis.

As regards the different forms of the attributes, it has to be noticed, that the occurrence of a preposition and a conjunction cause some difficulties. Look at the following sentences with free (F) and bound (B) attributes:

(8) Mozart wordt beschouwd als een van de grootste kunstenaars in de geschiedenis (B)
 (Mozart is considered as one of the greatest artists in history)
 Als een van de grootste kunstenaars in de geschiedenis zal Mozart onsterfelijk blijken. (F)
 (As one of the greatest artists in history Mozart will appear to be immortal).

What exactly is to be considered as the attribute: the constituent with *als* or the constituent behind that conjunction? The problem can be judged best in connection with the bound attribute. The choice is between the following reconstructions, both of which are given in active voice:

(9) men beschouwt als [S Mozart een van de grootste kunstenaars]
 men beschouwt [S Mozart als een van de grootste kunstenaars]

The conjunction *als* evidently cannot be motivated within the borders of the small clause; it has only sense in relation to the verb of the matrix[27]. It is not difficult to choose the first of both options. Inspired by this consideration, one feels inclined to make a paralleled choice for the analysis of a free attribute:

(10) Mozart zal als een van de grootste kunstenaars onsterfelijk blijken
 Mozart zal als [S PRO een van de grootste kunstenaars] onsterfelijk blijken.
 Mozart zal [S PRO als een van de grootste kunstenaars] onsterfelijk blijken.

I think the first idea is the better choice and the second reconstruction has to be discarded. In traditional grammar of Dutch, the use of the conjunction *als* in constructions like these, often is characterized as having an arguing function; it seems to be giving the ground on which the main contents of the statement is based. This can explain the use of *als* within the matrix. When, within the framework of CASUS, we decide to subordinate the small clause (without a PRO) to the NC with which it is associated semantically, we have to aim at a construction like:

(11) [NC Mozart [ATT als een van de grootste kunstenaars]] zal
onsterfelijk blijken.

An attribute with a preposition should get similar treatment. To recapitulate I give examples of proposed analyses in (12), both with conjunction and preposition:

(12) Men beschouwt Mozart als de grootste kunstenaar.
Men beschouwt Mozart als [S t de grootste kunstenaar]
Men beschouwt als [S Mozart de grootste kunstenaar]
Men beschouwt [ATT als de grootste kunstenaar [OBJ Mozart]]
Ik houd dat voor ongerechtvaardigd.
(I hold that for unjustified)
Ik houd dat voor [S t ongerechtvaardigd]
Ik houd voor [S dat ongerechtvaardigd]
Ik houd [ATT voor ongerechtvaardigd [OBJ dat]]

In both cases the last lines are suggestions for the semantic representations to be built by CASUS. I will return to that point below.

Up to this point no mention has been made about the third type of attributes, viz. those of (3). In connection with this type, it is less problematic than as regards (2), to claim that the matrix verb does not subcategorize an objective. Clear evidence concerning that point is given by the first example of (3), repeated in (13):

(13) Hij liep zijn voeten stuk.

since it need not be argued that *lopen* (to walk) is an intransitive verb. In connection with this type, it does not seem too hazardous to choose the same explanation for type (2).

As a next point, let us look to the question what are the possible places in surface structures for attributes to appear on, and in connection with that: how has to run the algorithm to decide with which constituents the bound and free attributes have to be connected. It would be better perhaps to ask on what places of the sentence a small clause with a PRO has to be generated, to admit coindexing with NC-i, if the sentence contains more than one NC. If a small clause with a trace is concerned: where should be the place of the small clause in order to decide that NC-i has been raised from it, if the sentence contains more than one NC. Put in another way: whith which NC has the trace and the PRO to be associated:

(14) NC NC NC [S t [A]]
NC NC NC [S PRO [A]]

In terms of sentence generation, the question concerns constraints on the place to which move-α may be directed, or, in the second instance, on the domain of the coindexing. For a clear discussion it may be suitable to first formulate my hypotheses:

(15) The trace concerns the apparent Objective of the matrix.
The PRO concerns the NC directly to the left.

Let us first look at an example with only a bound attribute and let us take constructions in the form of subclauses, in order to avoid secondary difficulties, raised by topicalization and WH-movement:

(16) ... hij muziek meestal lelijk vond
(... he music mostly ugly found)

In the hypothesis is spoken about an 'apparent objective'. I mean by that a constituent which would be detected as an objective, if the verb would be lexically marked as claiming an object with normal properties. Put in another way: the constituent meant behaves on the level of the matrix in all respects like an objective. In the example sentence this is the constituent *muziek*. Apart from secondary transformations, that constituent would be the last one in the sentence, if there were no bound attribute. The bound attribute is necessarily placed on the very end of the MI-part and the trace of it's small clause is associated with the first NC to the left, if this is not the subject or, in terms of cases, the agentive or dative. Thus, there seems to be no problem at all for a semantic interpreter to produce correct decisions.

To decide the interpretation of free attributes, we must beforehand touch upon a secondary problem, namely the use of a definite or an indefinite NC. Look at the following examples, again in subclause order:

(17) ik groente meestal ongekookt eet
* ik meestal groente ongekookt eet
(I mostly vegetables unboiled eat)

Since the ungrammaticalness of the second example is caused by the indefiniteness of the constituent *groente*, I will avoid the phenomenon in my analysis. Look at the following pair:

(18) ik de groente meestal ongekookt eet
ik meestal de groente ongekookt eet

Now it's possible to concentrate on examples with both a bound and a free attribute:

(19) ik de muziek vroeger altijd luid lelijk vond
ik vroeger altijd de muziek luid lelijk vond.
(I formerly always the music loud ugly found)

The question has to be raised: what is the correct interpretation of the free attribute *luid*? Is it impossible on syntactic grounds to connect it with *ik*? It might be a certain feature of the world that is an obstacle for that interpretation. We have to look for another example to judge that possibility:

(20) hij eenmaal geblondeerd zijn vriendin niet leuk meer vond
hij zijn vriendin eenmaal geblondeerd niet leuk meer vond
(he once blonded his girlfriend not pretty more found)

It seems to be impossible to connect *eenmaal geblondeerd* with *zijn vriendin* in the first example. However, it is not absolutely sure, that, in the second example, a connection of the attribute with *hij* has to be excluded. Look at an example that, because of a normal structure of reality, should be interpreted that way:

(21) hij zijn geweer, eenmaal volleerd jager geworden, nooit meer gebruikte
(he his rifle, once a perfect hunter become, never more used)

Nevertheless, it seems to be clear, that an association with an NC to the right is excluded and that a high preference exists for choosing the first NC in left direction. I add to that, that CASUS considers this as an obliged rule. There is one more point to pay attention to. The following sentence goes in order perfectly:

(22) Karel het papier enthousiast groen begon te verven
(Charles the paper enthusiastically green began to paint)

An easy and fully satisfying explanation is to consider *enthousiast* as an adverb and not as an attribute, connected with *Karel*. I conclude, that the hypothesis about the possible interpretation of attributes, as formulated in (15) is correct. The theory can even be generalised as follows:

(23) The attribute has to be associated semantically with th NC immediately to the left of it.

It should be noticed that the tag NC of a free attribute may not itself be a constituent of the matrix. Look at the observation:

(24) Wij horen van die man als redenaar veel goeds[28].
(We hear of that man as an orator much good)

The attribute *als redenaar* concerns the NC *die man*, which is a subconstituent of the PC *van die man*, which is at the level of the matrix.

It is theory (23) that was implemented in CASUS. I refer to section 3.2.1.11 (Testing a Case Frame), where the algorithm is dealt with in detail in relation to other aspects of the semantic interpretation.

The foregoing statements are refuted totally by an occasional topicalization or WH-movement, by which an attribute or some other sentence part is moved to the highest COMP position. These transformations typically change the sequence of the sentence parts and thus cause a conflict with the hypothesis (23). In order to let the algorithm operate correctly, the original sequence of the sentence parts will have to be restored. Since this problem is not specific for the subject under consideration and therefore better can be dealt with in a general section, I refer to 3.2.1.8 (The sequence of the Case Candidates), and confine myself at this moment to some example sentences that show the transformations meant:

(25) a. Hoe denk je dat hij het vond?
(How do you think that he it found?)
b. Voor wat denk je dat hij me uitmaakte?
(For what do you think that he railed at me?)
c. Als wat denk je dat ze hem benoemd hebben?
(As what do you think that they appointed him?).

The implementation of the attribute theory in CASUS made it necessary to change the set of case names, to specify lexical information for the attributes, claimed by different verbs, and to define redundancy rules for the default features of an attribute in cases where the lexicon does not specify any. A verb like *benoemen*, which claims an attribute in the form of a PC with preposition *tot* and an agentive is lexically marked in the following way:

(26) AGE(),ATT(/PC/tot),*

which means: an agentive with default features and an attribute in the form mentioned just now. Note, that a free attribute never is claimed by a lexical specification, since it is typically an optional sentence part.

As an illustration, I give the AMAZON structures and the SELANCA expressions for the sentences of (27) in the diagrams of (28):

(27) Ik heb muziek altijd luid lelijk gevonden.
Ik heb muziek altijd lelijk gevonden.

(28)

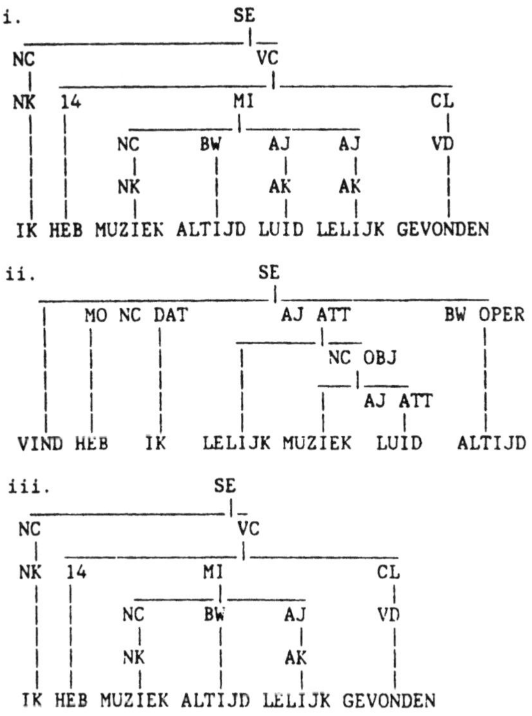

```
iv.                       SE
      ____________________|_______________
      |  MO NC DAT         AJ ATT     BW OPER
      |  |     |          __|__          |
      |  |     |          |  NC OBJ      |
      |  |     |          |     |        |
   VIND HEB   IK    LELIJK MUZIEK   ALTIJD

v.                        SE
      ____________________|_______________
      |  MO NC AGE         NC OBJ     BW OPER
      |  |     |          __|__          |
      |  |     |          |  AJ ATT      |
      |  |     |          |     |        |
   VIND HEB   IK    MUZIEK LELIJK   ALTIJD
```

I notice, that only the AMAZON structure with the interpretation 'adjective' for both *luid* and *lelijk* is regarded. The interpretation of the sentence shown in (28)i. is given in (28)ii. There is a dative function assigned to *Ik*, a bound attribute function assigned to *lelijk* and, associated with this attribute, an object *muziek*, to which, on it's turn, the free attribute *luid* is connected. The interpretation is correct and fully in accord with the foregoing explanation. Sentence (28)iii. gets two different semantic interpretations, (28)iv and (28)v. The first is of the same type as (28)ii. The second interpretation makes use of the case frame with agentive and concrete objective. The word *lelijk* is considered now as a free attribute, related with *muziek*. The sentence, in this reading, means: I have always found music while it was in an ugly state. I think the interpretation cannot be discarded on linguistic grounds.

(29) Patrick probeerde Lucie leuk te vinden.

(30)

```
                          SE
      ____________________|__________
      |      NC AGE            W2 OBJ
      |         |        __________|______
      |         |        |  NC DAT     AJ ATT
      |         |        |     |       __|__
      |         |        |     |       |  NC OBJ
      |         |        |     |       |     |
   PROBEER PATRICK VIND   PRO  LEUK  LUCIE

                          SE
      ____________________|__________
      |      NC AGE            W2 OBJ
      |         |        __________|______
      |         |        |  NC DAT     AJ ATT
      |         |        |     |       __|__
      |         |        |     |       |  NC OBJ
      |         |        |     |       |     |
   PROBEER  LUCIE  VIND   PRO  LEUK PATRICK
```

Although we did not speak yet about S complements, a certain difficulty has to be mentioned concerning the interaction of the algorithms for attributes and raising phenomena. In a sentence like (29) all the constituents appear on one and the same syntactic surface level and, consequently, the attribute *leuk* automatically will be tested within the environment of *probeer*.

(31) Leuk probeerde Patrick Lucie te vinden.
(Patrick tried to find Lucy cute.)

```
i.                        SE
      ____________________|_______
      |       NC AGE            W2 OBJ
      |         |        _______|______
      |         |        |  NC DAT      AJ ATT
      |         |        |    |          __|__
      |         |        |    |         |  NC OBJ
      |         |        |    |         |     |
PROBEER PATRICK VIND    PRO   LEUK  LUCIE
```

```
ii.                       SE
      ____________________|_______
      |       NC AGE            W2 OBJ
      |         |        _______|______
      |         |        |  NC AGE      NC OBJ
      |         |        |    |          __|__
      |         |        |    |         |  AJ ATT
      |         |        |    |         |     |
PROBEER PATRICK VIND    PRO   LUCIE  LEUK
```

```
iii.                     SE
      ___________________|_______
      |       NC AGE          W2 OBJ
      |         |        _____|__________
      |         |        |   NC AGE   NC OBJ
      |         |        |  ___|__       |
      |         |        | |  AJ ATT     |
      |         |        | |     |       |
PROBEER PATRICK VIND PRO  LEUK   LUCIE
```

It will be clear, that this method will yield unwanted semantic interpretations. What we would prefer is, that on the highest level only the constituent *Patrick* appears and in the complement a PRO, *Lucie* and *leuk*. In order to have these interpretations produced by CASUS, the rule was added that an attribute never may be assigned to a constituent of the matrix if an S complement with raising is present. The interpretations of (29) under that rule are given in (30). For convenience sake I confine myself to the instances with the interpretation of *vinden* (to find) as an attribute claiming verb. It should be noticed that also attaching of an attribute to a PRO constituent in the S complement is performed correctly in cases where this is wanted. This is illustrated by sentence (31) with it's SELANCA representations, shown in the same figure. Note that different case frames of *vinden* are used for these interpretations; the case AGE indicates the meaning 'to find something while looking for it', the case DAT 'to have a certain opinion about something'.

### 3.2.1.8 THE SEQUENCE OF THE CASE CANDIDATES

The semantic functions of the constituents of a construction can only be decided by a rule that predicts those functions on the basis of their formal properties. The set of properties that may be taken into açcount is: syntactic features, lexical semantic feature information and position. The problem with respect to a constituent that has been moved is typically, that the information about it's original position is lost. If all information about syntactic state, semantic features and position is available, a conclusion about the semantic function must be attainable, since no information of another kind is at hand and our hypothesis must be that a natural language sentence is interpretable anyhow. The problem of semantic interpretation of moved constituents is the question of their original place.

Let us first look at the interpretation of sentence constituents in an undisturbed situation. Our hypothesis is, that the case functions claimed by a verb are realized in a certain sequence and that this sequence is:

(1) AGE - DAT - INS - OBJ - FAC - LOC - ATT

As a matter of fact, this hypothesis cannot be falsified independently, since it is related with an undisturbed situation and this itself is to be related with a theory about moving. Another reason is, that no verb will claim all possible cases, so that never a situation will occur where the whole row of (1) may be observed. The hypothesis is to be understood in the following way: never will the cases, claimed by a verb and occurring in a construction about which no previous moving of a constituent is hypothesized, be in conflict with the order of (1). It should be noticed already now, that in (1) the occurrence of optional parts as adverbs of time and place etc. is unaccounted for.

The theory about WH-movement in an analyzing model specifies the different S constructions where a certain WH-constituent may have been generated. We dealt with that question in section 3.2.1.5. That theory does not decide itself which S construction has to be regarded as the correct one. This has to be done by the semantic theory strictly speaking, which is founded upon knowledge about the semantic features of the verbs and which is therefore able to judge the semantic plausibility of what is possible syntactically. This semantic decision, however, needs something more than only the information that a WH-constituent may have been generated in a certain S construction, connected with the subcategorization rules of the verb. Since the moved constituent is moved to the COMP position of the original S first and only afterwards to the higher COMP's, it is necessary to also reconstruct the exact place in the construction where the WH-constituent was generated, in order to decide about it's semantic function. The subject of this section is that exact original place and the way how it is found by the algorithm.

A first possible way to solve the problem might be to handle the case candidates of a certain verb in the order they are met in surface structure, supposing that a lowered WH-constituent is situated in the first position. The candidates could be processed by the interpreter by testing the case functions, claimed by the verb, in some special order. Obviously, this process would have to be directed by knowledge about the possible order in which the different case functions may be distributed over the case candidates, i.e. something like (1). It is not to be deemed impossible that this process could work, but it seems to be rather difficult if it is intended to account for possible ambiguities. For this way to perform the interpretation, I refer to Van Bakel [1982]. The version of CASUS, used at that time, worked with a grammar of sequences, which was defined separately (which means: outside the computer program) and read in by CASUS for every run. The grammar contained rules of the form:

(2) DB , SU , SU I-> (A D O , O A D) .

The meaning was: if on a certain syntactic level three constituents are met, the first being a DB (the relative pronoun *die*), the second and the third a SU (a substantive with the feature +ANI), try to interpret the construction with the hypothesis 'A D O' (which means: the first is the agentive, the second the dative and the third the objective) and afterwards with the hypothesis 'O A D'. The actual test was performed after resetting the sequence of case functions to be tested (not the case candidates) in such a way that is was in accordance with the specification of the rule concerned. For all possibly ambiguous sequences of case candidates, rules of this type were contained in the grammar. Clearly, these rules seemed to be rather ad hoc, and it was rather obscure how generalizations could be expressed in rules of this type. The rules had almost no grammatical state. They defined a way to find a solution rather than a theory about movement. If a sentence should start with the words *wie ik* ..., a rule said: try the case functions dative and agentive in this order and afterwards objective and agentive and objective and dative. Linguistically spoken, only knowledge about a possible use of *wie* and *ik* was used for it, but no intuition about possible sequences of case functions. But the semantic interpretation worked fine, and some new experiences should have to be met in order for me to be able to distinguish the restrictions. These were detected while working on the theory of interpreting attributes (see section 3.2.1.7). If the WH-constituent is itself an attribute, rules like (2) are difficult to build, since an attribute is related to another case candidate, rather than being an autonomous candidate with it's own place itself. Look at the function of *luid* (loud) in the following sentence:

(3) Luid vind ik muziek lelijk.
(Loud find I music ugly)
I do not like music being played loudly.

Note by the way, that the semantic ambiguities of the sentence are lost in the translation. The first sentence part, *luid*, may concern both *ik* and *muziek*, but it is impossible to find out what are possible places for the attribute without examining the features of other constituents of the construction.

This was the reason to look for another way to tackle the problem and the following was found. A constituent that has been moved to the complementizer position is one of the case candidates, so it has to meet the claims for at least one of the cases which are claimed by the verb. It is possible to test which case role can be played by that constituent. If it is, say, the role of the objective, we have to investigate what is the sequence number of that function in the set of cases, claimed for the verb by its's lexical entry. If the objective should appear to be the second case of the verb, it may be concluded that the moved constituent will have to be positioned at the second place in the row. If the cases are tested in one fixed order, the objective will be tested as the second function. Look at the following example:

(4) Candidates: wat, hij (zei)
(what , he (said))
Cases claimed; AGE(), OBJ(+ABS)
*Wat* meets the claims for the objective.
Sequence to test: hij, wat

This test will succeed and the method applied has to be considered adequate. If the moved constituent should meet the claims for more than one case function, the sentence may be ambiguous and the test will have to be repeated for other sequences. Note, that the ambiguity can not be fully detected by looking only at the moved constituent; the features of other constituents could disambiguate it. Anyhow, a second test will have to consider another case function with the candidate put on the corresponding place in between the other candidates. This seems to be sufficient to honour all of the different readings of a sentence.

However, the method is not suitable to decide all situations. Principally when an attribute is moved to the complementizer position, things become very difficult, since it may function both as a free and as a bound sentence part (the reader should refer to section 3.2.1.7 for this subject) and a free attribute may have to be related with a set of constituents which is difficult to define in general terms. It may concern even an NC that is not present at the level of the construction but is embedded somewhere; look at example (24) of section 3.2.1.7. Whatever might be the result of an investigation about possible hypothetical places of an attribute, it is quite sure that the attribute would claim a separate treatment. Thus, also this second method, considered at the moment, does not seem to be very attractive.

A third proposal might be called a jack-screw. That is a nice instrument because of it's power, but it is suspect, since it is likely to be too mighty for it's purpose. The problem need not only be solved, but should be solved adequately. The idea is: the constituent has been generated somewhere, so try to interpret it on all places where it possibly comes from. This means that, if the construction shows *n* candidates, the moved candidate should be tested on *n* different places. Although the method has some disadvantages, I used it, because it seems to be better than all the others. In addition, the approach is based on the simple intuition that a constituent that has been moved to COMP, may have been generated on every place of the construction. The example analysis, shown in the appendix, illustrates what is meant. An insufficiency of this approach is the following. If a construction contains, apart from, say, two candidates for a verb's case functions, two operators, one of which is moved to the complementizer position, CASUS will produce four identical semantic interpretations:

(5) waarom hij gisteren beweerde dat het niet kon
(why he yesterday said that it not could;
...why he said yesterday that it was not possible)
hij ; gisteren ; dat(x) ; waarom
hij ; gisteren ; waarom ; dat(x)
hij ; waarom ; gisteren ; dat(x)
waarom ; hij ; gisteren ; dat(x)

According to the idea formulated, the algorithm should yield four permutations, while only one semantic interpretation seems to be wanted. A way to prevent unwanted interpretations is to have the assigning of functions controlled by a severe order of testing. As soon as the claims of a certain case function tested should not be met by the candidate considered, the test of this special permutation should be regarded fallacious immediately. This restriction has indeed been used, as is shown by scheme (1) in section 3.2.1.11. The restriction, however, does not work in the example (5), since it is necessary to admit an operator to occur in between case candidates, as is illustrated by (6):

(6) Hij schreef de laatste jaren veel korte verhalen
(He wrote the last years many short stories)

where the factitive is preceded by a temporal operator. Therefore, at least in some instances an operator should be hypothesized before all case functions are fulfilled. That is a reason to hypothesize more than one original place for the operator *waarom* in (5), although not four different places should be presupposed. The difficulty, however, is not caused by to many hypotheses but by to many solutions. Even if more than one hypothesis seems to be acceptable with respect to the original place of *waarom*, there is a rather weighty objection to an idea of semantic ambiguity: construction (5) has only one meaning.

As long as no better hypothesis about the original places of moved constituents is available, the four solutions for (5) cannot easily be avoided. There seems to be only one possibility to restrict the number of semantic interpretations, namely the ad hoc rule saying: a moved operator has been generated on the last place of the construction. Although this rule is not accounted for by the scheme (1) in section 3.2.1.11, the algorithm of the subroutine 'Applicable structure' uses it. It also uses the severe rule about sequence while testing the case functions defined in a verb's case frame. This is shown in the example analysis in section 4 of the appendix[29].

Some remarks have to be made about the part of the algorithm which decides whether the set of case candidates has to be considered under several hypotheses about their order. Only when the verb under consideration appears in a WH bridge or when topicalization has occurred, that condition may be met. To fully specify the cases when and when not different hypotheses should be tested, I refer to figure (7) in connection with which some explanations might be wellcome. If an originally passive construction is met, there is no possible ambiguity, since the original PC with preposition *door* (by), changed into an NC, or the dummy are the only candidates for the agentive, so the case candidates should only be considered in the order they are met. (That is the meaning of the index '1' that is shown at the bottom.) I refer to section 3.2.1.3. The same is the case, if the structure is a main clause, showing the interrogative form (a yes/no question). If a main clause is met in another form, there should be made a distinction between cases of WH-movement, indicated in the scheme by 'Bridge verb', and others. The last group is divided in relative subclauses and others. The union of a certain subset of the first and one of the second group is submitted to the test whether currently a frame is considered under the hypothesis that the WH-constituent plays a semantic role at 'this' sentence level. In special situations, the investigation is made whether the first case candidate is an operator.

(7)

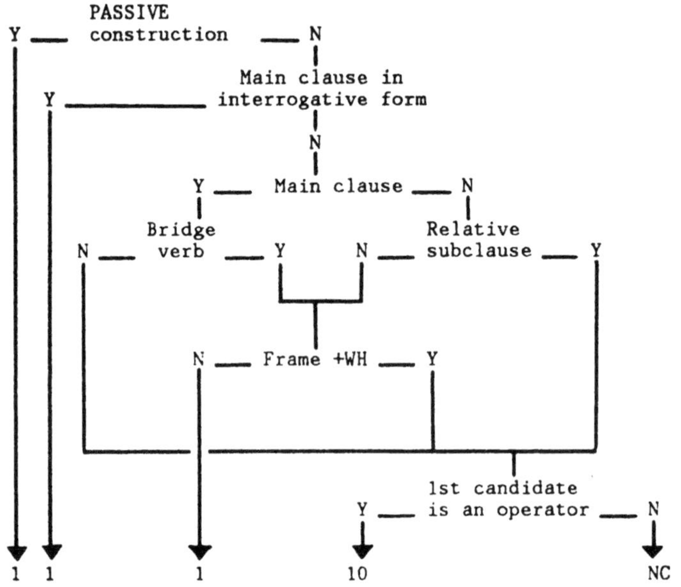


The result '10' means: assume that the first case candidate is generated on the last place of the construction. 'NC' (Number of candidates) means: test subsequently the hypotheses that the first constituent is generated behind case candidate *i* for every candidate of the construction. In section 4 of the appendix messages are included about these tests. In a construction with *i* case candidates, the first test to be performed is that with the position behind candidate i, the next one behind candidate *i* minus 1, etc. These values of *i* are also displayed in section 4 of the the appendix.

To conclude this section, I give a somewhat shortened tracing of the semantic interpretation by CASUS of an example sentence:

(8) Waarom heeft Karel gezegd dat hij kwam?
(Why has Charles said that he came?)

The tracing is not postedited. It shows details about the testing of different sequences of the case candidates.

WAAROM HEEFT KAREL GEZEGD DAT HIJ KWAM.
Verb No. 1 GEZEGD
1 : GEZEGD
Change sequence cases 10
1 Case Candidates * (NC(NK-KAREL))

2 Case Candidates * (CC(VW-DAT)(W1-(MI-(NC-(NK-HIJ)))(CL-(PV-KOM))))
3 Case Candidates * (BW WAAROM)
> GEZEGD Analysis succeeds:
(SE-(VC-(CL-(VD-ZEG(MO-(14-HEB))(NC AGE-(NK-KAREL))(CC OBJ-(VW-DAT-
)(W1 -(MI-(NC-(NK-HIJ)))(CL-(PV-KOM))))(BW OPER-WAAROM)))(MI-)(UL-)))##

Verb No. 2 KWAM
1 : KWAM
2 : KWAM
Change sequence cases 1
1 Case Candidates * (NC(NK-HIJ))
> KWAM Analysis succeeds:
(SE-(VC-(CL-(VD-ZEG(MO-(14-HEB))(NC AGE-(NK-KAREL))(CC OBJ-(VW-DAT-
)(W1
-(MI-)(CL-(PV-KOM(NC AGE-(NK-HIJ))))))(BW OPER-WAAROM)))(MI-)(UL-)))##

Verb No. 1 GEZEGD
2 : GEZEGD
Change sequence cases 1
1 Case Candidates * (NC(NK-KAREL))
2 Case Candidates * (CC(VW-DAT)(W1-(CL-(PV-KOM(NC AGE-(NK-HIJ))))))
> GEZEGD Analysis succeeds:
(SE-(VC-(CL-(VD-ZEG(MO-(14-HEB))(NC AGE-(NK-KAREL))(CC OBJ-(VW-DAT-
)(W1 -(CL-(PV-KOM(NC AGE-(NK-HIJ))))))))))##

Verb No. 2 KWAM
1 : KWAM
Change sequence cases 10
1 Case Candidates * (NC(NK-HIJ))
2 Case Candidates * (BW WAAROM)
> KWAM Analysis succeeds:
(SE-(VC-(CL-(VD-ZEG(MO-(14-HEB))(NC AGE-(NK-KAREL))(CC OBJ-(VW-DAT-
)(W1 -(CL-(PV-KOM(NC AGE-(NK-HIJ))(BW OPER-WAAROM)))))))))##

2 : KWAM
Change sequence cases 1
1 Case Candidates * (NC(NK-HIJ))
> KWAM Analysis succeeds:
(SE-(VC-(CL-(VD-ZEG(MO-(14-HEB))(NC AGE-(NK-KAREL))(CC OBJ-(VW-DAT-
)(W1 -(CL-(PV-KOM(NC AGE-(NK-HIJ))))))))))##

Verb No. 1 GEZEGD
3 : GEZEGD
Analysis fails.

The two semantic interpretations of (8), presented by the tracing in labeled bracketings are (9):

(9)

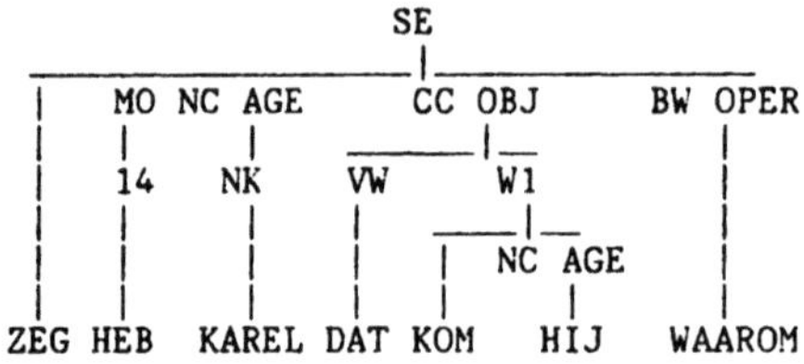
SE
MO NC AGE
CC OBJ
BW OPER
14
NK
VW
W1
NC AGE
ZEG HEB KAREL DAT KOM HIJ WAAROM

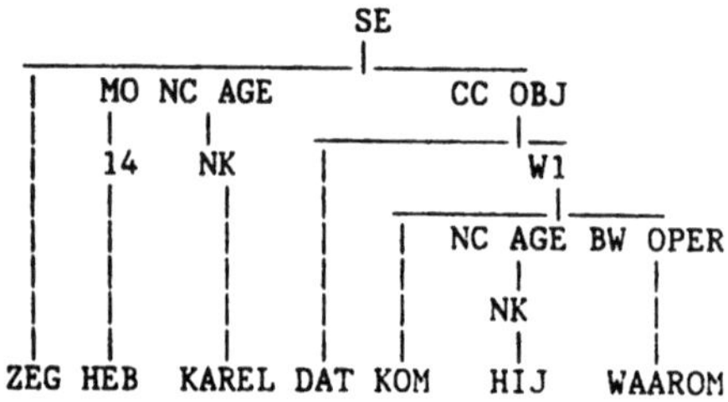
SE
MO NC AGE
CC OBJ
14
NK
W1
NC AGE BW OPER
NK
ZEG HEB KAREL DAT KOM HIJ WAAROM

### 3.2.1.9 INTERPRETING S-COMPLEMENTS

In this section we deal with semantic interpretation of S-complements. In describing this part of CASUS, I will use the familiar terminology, used generally for that subject in linguistic theory. Global reference may be made to Chomsky [1981]. I will assume that the main ideas and terminology of that study are known to the reader. Special difficulties will be met in connection with S-complements, namely: 1) specifying the empty (absent) constituent(s) of the complement and it's/their semantic function; 2) bringing back into the complement those constituents that have been raised from there; 3) unravel the clustering of the verbs of the matrix and the S-complement. In dealing with these subjects I will distinguish the following verb categories: the type *besluiten* (to decide), the type *bevelen* (to order), the type *horen* (to hear) and the type *schijnen* (to seem). Let us first characterize these different types.

(1) i. BESLUITEN (lexical type: SUC - subject control)
Ik besloot mij erbuiten te houden
(I decided to keep out)
Ik besloot [ PRO (=ik) mij erbuiten te houden.

ii. BEVELEN (lexical type: IOC - indirect object control)
Cecile beval mij me erbuiten te houden
(Cecile ordered me to keep out)
Cecile beval mij [ PRO (=mij) me erbuiten te houden.

iii. HOREN (lexical type: RTO - raising to object)
Patrick hoorde Lucie Bach zingen
(Patrick heard Lucy sing Bach)
Patrick hoorde [ t (=Lucie) Bach zingen.

iv. SCHIJNEN (lexical type: RTS - raising to subject)
Lucie schijnt Bach te zingen
(Lucy seems to sing Bach)
Lucie schijnt [ t (=Lucie) Bach te zingen.

All Dutch verbs that cause one or more of the above mentioned difficulties in relation with S-complements can be brought into one of these four types. Let me try to characterize them globally.

i. The type 'Besluiten' shows a PRO constituent, which has to function semantically as the agentive (or dative) of the main verb of the complement. This PRO has to be associated (by coindexing) with the constituent of the matrix that functions semantically as the agentive.
ii. The type 'Bevelen' also shows a PRO in it's complement construction. That

PRO functions as an agentive (or dative). It has to be associated, however, with the constituent of the matrix that functions as the dative.
iii. The complement of the type 'Horen' shows a trace constituent, which has been left there after the moving of the agentive to an NC position of the matrix. The moved (raised) constituent does not function semantically in the matrix, but has the superficial features of a kind of objective.
iv. The type 'Schijnen' is very much the same as 'horen'. The only difference is, that the moved constituent behaves like an agentive (subject) in the matrix.

In order to understand what exactly are the difficulties for semantic interpretation, we have to deal with matters of verb raising first. Consider the sentences (2) with their AMAZON-structures (3):

(2) i. Eric heeft alweer geprobeerd zijn vingers te bewegen
ii. Eric heeft zijn vingers alweer proberen te bewegen
(Eric has already tried (again) to move his fingers (again)).

(3) I.

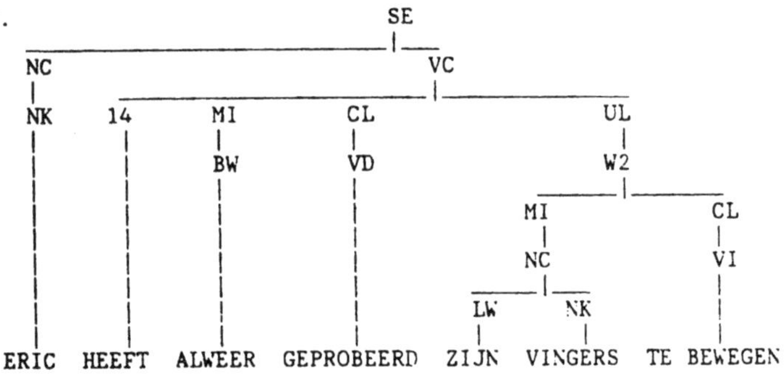


ii.

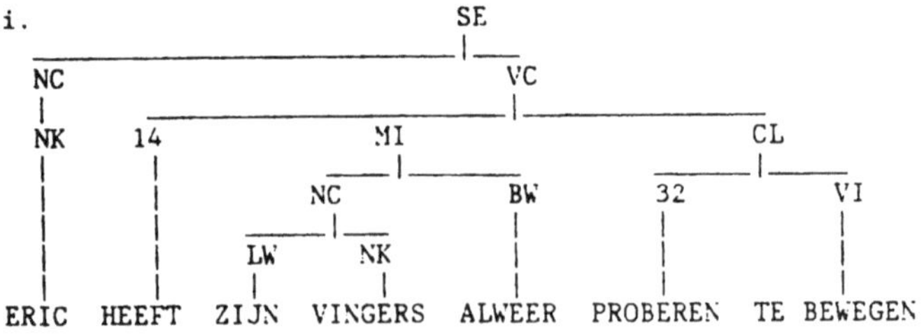


The analysis of (3)ii is highly dependent upon the choice the user of AMAZON makes in answer to a question about the lexical categories to assign to *proberen*. If he should choose 'vsubi' (i.e. main verb in the form infinitive; cfr. (4) in section 2.1), the sentence would get no analysis from AMAZON. I will not go into details about the reason of that; it may be found out by the reader by consulting the first section of the appendix. On the basis of the choice 'hvtii' (auxiliary claiming an infinitive plus *te* in the form of an infinitive) the verbal cluster *heeft proberen te bewegen* is considered as an acceptable combination. The interpretation implies, that the verb of the S-complement (which construction itself is not recognized by AMAZON as such) has chosen a surface position in the same verbal environment where also *proberen* resides. The situation in surface structure is characterized by the fact that the clustering of the verbal forms is similar to that of a main verb connected with one or more auxiliaries. Such a cluster is unpenetrable, since nothing can be put in between[30]. This is a reason to consider verbs like *proberen* and other verbs that cause verb raising as semi-auxiliaries. It is shown that AMAZON is able to assign an acceptable syntactic structure to a construction that is the result of what is known as verb raising in transformational theory. Sentence (3)ii differs typically from sentence (3)i in showing the raising of *te bewegen* to the level of *proberen*. By entering the matrix, the verb of the complement urges the main verb of that level (*proberen*) to behave like an auxiliary. Note by the way, that structure (3)i does not show any specific feature that would be relevant in the present discussion. As will be argued below, we will even have to discard it as incorrect. Note also, that the form *geprobeerd* is not ambiguous, since a past participle never can be.

Let us see how the sentences of (1) behave when a verb raising situation is created which is comparable with the structure of (3)ii.

(4) i. Ik heb besloten mij erbuiten te houden.
* Ik heb mij erbuiten besluiten te houden.
ii. Cecile heeft mij bevolen mij erbuiten te houden.
* Cecile heeft mij me erbuiten bevelen te houden.
iii. * Ik heb gehoord Lucie Bach te zingen.
Ik heb Lucie Bach horen zingen.
iv. * Lucie heeft geschenen Bach te zingen.
Lucie heeft Bach schijnen te zingen.

It appears that the four types mentioned differ from each other in an interesting way as to the possibility to attract the verb of the complement to their own level (verb raising). The verb *proberen*, when compared with the observations of (4), appears to represent a new type by showing both structures, with and without verb raising, which are never found together in any other type considered.

As has been suggested already, verb raising is mainly to be characterized as a kind of mixing of the contents of different verbal constructions on the level of the highest one of both. In the surface structures of sentences that show verb raising (and others[31]) it is impossible to draw the borderline between what should be considered to belong to the different syntactic levels originally. Let us examine again the sentences of (1) in this connection. Transparant borders between complement and matrix exist there also. In (1)ii (not showing verb raising) the constituent *mij*, regarding the matrix, and *me* and *erbuiten*, regarding the complement, may appear in different MI-parts, irrespective their original places. Something has to be said about the way AMAZON deals whith that problem. As an example let us take the sentence:

(5) Ik probeerde Jan gisteren een boek te verkopen
(I tried John yesterday a book to buy)
Yesterday I tried to buy a book to John.

As to the lexical category of *probeerde* it has to be noted, that, by the form of sentence (5), it is accidentally so, that choosing the category of both auxiliary (hvtip) and main verb (vsubp) yield AMAZON analyses. The first choice implies that the infinitive *te verkopen* has to appear under CL and, by consequence, al three intervening parts under MI of VC. No other interpretations are possible. Look at (6):

(6)

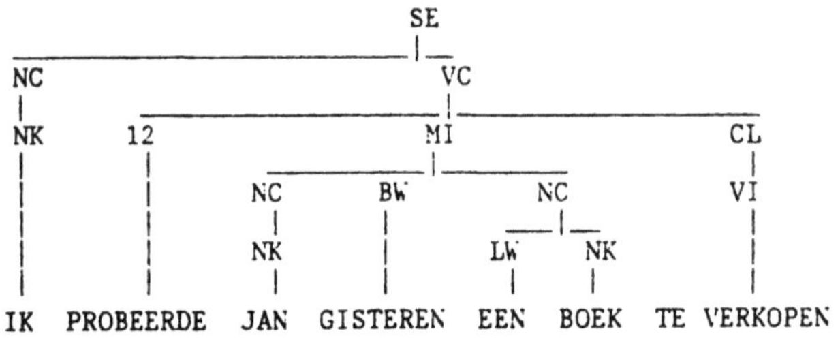


The choice of main verb, however, yields four different AMAZON structures. One of them is not interesting and will be skipped in (7); it is the structure with the interpretation of *gisteren een boek te verkopen* as a postmodifier of an NC with the noun *Jan* as a head. I leave it to the reader to think about that solution. The three other interpretations are:

(7)

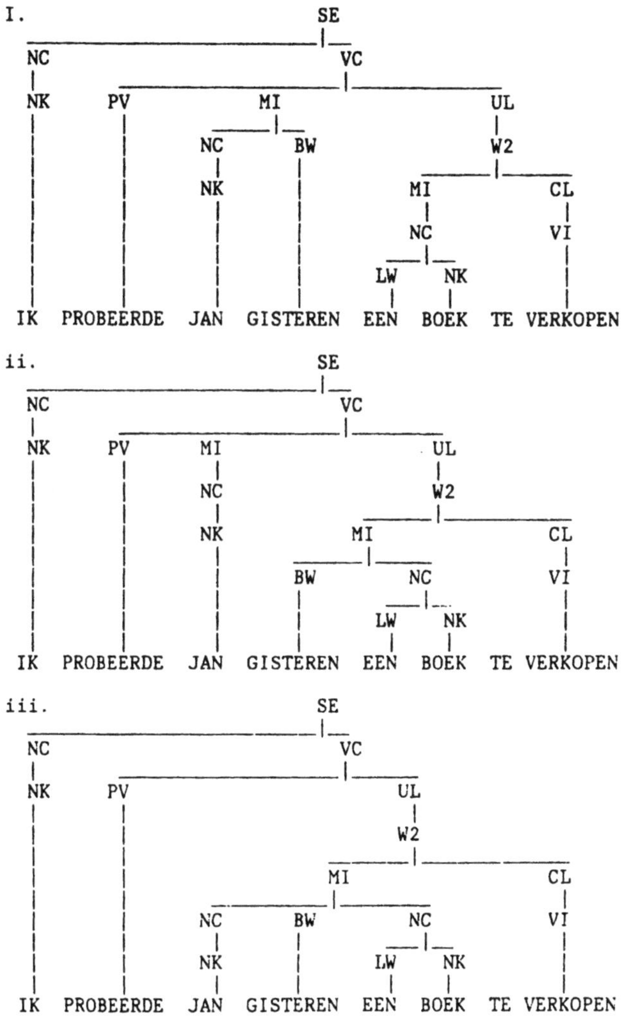


Since two different MI-parts (in the sense of rule (35); see section 1 of the appendix) are adjacent to each other, the set of three MI-constituents will be spread over them in all different possible ways, illustrating very convincingly what is said about the transparant border between complement and matrix. Structures like (7), however, are not very well in accordance with common theory about S-complements: the claims about features of surface structure are not met, since the characteristic clustering of the verbs is not visible. The autonomous W2 construction should typically be lost, since it is conflicting with the idea of the mixing of two different syntactic levels, which is suggested by the term *raising*. I will return to this point instantly.

The main subject of the present section is, of course, to answer the question how CASUS treats the structures of different S-complements and their matrices in order to adequately interpret semantically both the matrix and the complement. It will be clear that the following will have to be done: 1. the reconstruction of verb raising, 2. the reconstruction of raising of certain constituents from an S-complement, 3. the interpretation of PRO. The analysis and the implementation in CASUS were performed in cooperation with Toon van Opstal and Patrick Wever; parts of the work were reported earlier in Van Opstal [1983] and Wever [1984].

**Lowering of the verb**

Let us first look at the way the verb raising is undone in CASUS by what may be called verb lowering, a transformation that is the inverse of raising, and let us take as a typical example the AMAZON structures (7)iii and (6), repeated here as (8):

(8)

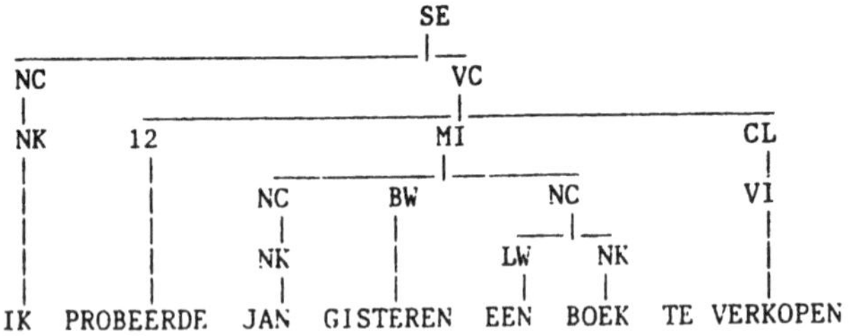


It will be clear that both constructions, (7)iii and (8), have totally different meanings as regards undoing verb raising. Structure (7)iii does not show a mixing of both levels. The choice of 'vsubp' for *probeert* urges AMAZON to distinguish two different syntactic levels, since two main verbs are never admitted to reside on one and the same sentence level and the verb *te verkopen* is necessarily to be considered as a main verb. Thus, only the construction (8) has to be dealt with in connection with verb raising. In (6-7), four different AMAZON structures appeared to be yielded on the basis of one dutch sentence. It is not acceptable to reduce this number by forbidding the choice of 'vsubp' (main verb in finite verb form), since this would imply the impossibility to parse a sentence like (2)i, where the choice of the category main verb is obligatory. Of course, also a kind of gentleman's agreement with the user that never the choice 'vsubp' should be made when 'hvtip' (auxiliary, claiming *te* plus infinitive, in the form of a finite verb) would also work, is unacceptable. Not what a user does is important, but what has been defined in the model. A way has to be found to warrant that no more than one semantic interpretation may be obtained from CASUS for the four structures of (6-7). I think the following consideration brings a solution. It follows from the observations, given in (2) and (4), that a sentence with a past participle never shows verb raising neither a mixing of constituents on two different sentence levels. Hence, these sentences will stay out of the problem considered at the moment. All other sentences, showing verbs with raising complements (the types of (4)iii and (4)iv and the representatives of the type *proberen*), which received an AMAZON structure like (7) are discarded, since the mixing, required by the theory, is not attested in the surface structure. If the surface structure does show the mixing, the sentence is accepted in principle and will be subjected to lowering as described in the context of (9) and (10). The reader will not fail to see, that this formulation implies a general theoretic concern, but is in fact parallel with stating that an interpretation with main verbs (as in (7)) is unacceptable.

Although we ought to distinguish constructions with and without clustering of verbs earlier, it will not be needed to do so as regards (8): we depart from the situation that the resetting of V has taken place and the forms *probeert* and *te verkopen* are collected under one CL-node (Cfr. section 3.2.1.2). See (9). If a cluster of the sentence appears to contain a semi-auxiliary (in this case *probeert*[32]), the remaining verbal forms are detached from the CL node and collected as sons in a new CL-node, which is attached to a W2-node, which is attached to an UL-node, which is attached to the VC-node under which the original CL-node was residing. See, for some clarification, the resulting situation in (10), where the original S-complement has become visible. The lowering, however, of some constituents that originally belonged to that complement but which have been raised to the matrix apparently, has still to be performed.

(9)

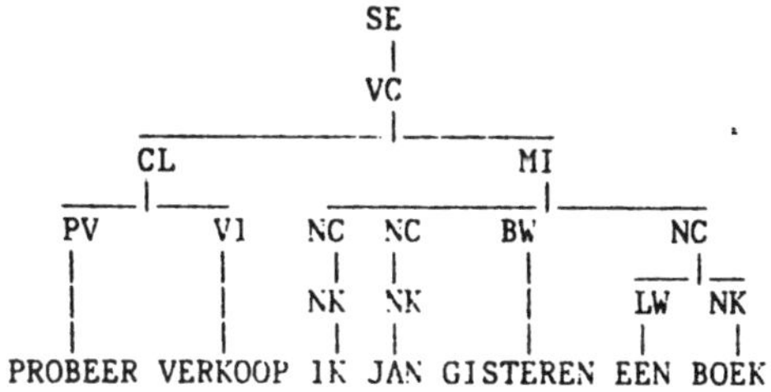

(10)

```
                          SE
                          |
                          VC
                          |
     ---------------------|---------------------
     CL                   MI                   UL
     |          ----------|----------           |
     PV    NC    NC       BW        NC         W2
     |     |     |        |        _|_          |
     |     NK    NK       |      LW    NK      CL
     |     |     |        |      |     |        |
     |     |     |        |      |     |       VI
     |     |     |        |      |     |        |
PROBEER   IK   JAN   GISTEREN   EEN  BOEK  VERKOOP
```

**Lowering of Sentence Constituents**

Lowering of constituents can only be performed if it is known where they belong. In other words, we will have to discover on which sentence level a certain constituent has been generated. As may be seen in (10), the higher level may contain in one transparant domain constituents that should be assigned to different sentence levels. Because of the transparancy of the border between the two levels in surface structures, AMAZON is not able to distribute the constituents over the different levels correctly. A solution has to be found nevertheless. If it were unattainable, no adequate theory about understanding these sentences would be possible. Look at the sentence (11):

(11) Jan probeert al dagen weer zijn knie te buigen.
(John tries already days again his knee to bow)
John tries for some days to bow his knee again.

The constituent *al dagen* should be assigned to the higher verb, *weer* and *zijn knie* to the lower. The place where the constituents are positioned by AMAZON seems to bear no information at all about their original level. Apparently, we have to decide the problem on the basis of an ambiguous surface structure. It has to be noticed that the problem only exists in constructions with verb raising. For that matter, look at (12):

(12) Jan heeft al dagen geprobeerd zijn knie weer te buigen.
Jan heeft al dagen weer geprobeerd zijn knie te buigen.

Obviously, there is no problem at all in this example: no verb raising has taken place and, as a consequence, no raising of sentence constituents either. The constituents of both verbal structures are neatly separated in surface structure. No special theory whatsoever is needed in this situation.

The observation (12), however, may hint at a solution for (11), looked for just now. If we compare the following sentences (13):

(13) a. Jan heeft al dagen weer zijn knie proberen te buigen
b. Jan heeft al dagen zijn knie weer proberen te buigen

it may be remarked that (13)a and (13)b match with (14)a and (14)b respectively:

(14) a. Jan heeft al dagen weer geprobeerd zijn knie te buigen
b. Jan heeft al dagen geprobeerd zijn knie weer te buigen.

The conclusion is, that at least some constraints are at work as to the possible sequence of sentence parts, being brougt together on one sentence level. The following rules can be postulated: 1. never can the raised constituents be put at the left of the constituents of the higher level[33]; 2. never can the order of the constituents of the lower level be changed by raising. This means that the set of gathered constituents on the higher level has after raising the structure:

(15) [basic order of constituents-1] [basic order of constituents-2]

where the first set belongs to the higher level and the second to the lower level originally. As soon as it is known how many constituents are claimed by the higher verb and how many by the lower, and what are the rules to define the order in which the constituents of one only level may appear, it seems to be possible to assign all constituents to semantic functions of the verbs of both levels.

Let the algorithm run in the folowing way: try to assign the different constituents, met on the level of the first verb, to semantic functions of that verb and, as soon as no functions are left, lower the constituent to the next level. In the example (13)a, the constituents *al dagen* and *weer*, although not being case function candidates but rather operators, may be assigned to the level of the hihgest verb *proberen*. As soon as *zijn knie* is met, there will be no possibility to assign it to a semantic function and the constituent will have to be lowered. In (13)b, the switch to the second level will have to be made in connection with *zijn knie* also, and consequently, according to (15), also *weer* will have to be lowered. This seems to be a correct way to proceed.

However, some difficulties still may rise. For that matter, look at the following observations:

(16) a. Peter heeft al dagenlang Mariet luidkeels Bach horen zingen.
(For some days Peter has heard Mariet sing Bach loudly.)

b. Peter heeft al dagenlang luidkeels Bach horen zingen.
c. Peter heeft al dagenlang luidkeels Mariet horen zingen.
d. Peter heeft al dagenlang Bach luidkeels horen zingen.
e. Peter heeft Mariet al dagenlang luidkeels horen zingen.

It is clear that in (16)a *Mariet* may only be interpreted as the agens of *zingen* and *Bach* as it's objective. The operator *al dagenlang* in this example has to be considered as belonging to the highest verb, since it should be positioned behind the subject of the S-complement if it were a part of that construction. See (16)e and cfr. also the discussion in connection with (13) and (14). In (16)b the constituent *Bach* is clearly the objective of the S-complement. Only if we interpret both *al dagenlang* and *luidkeels* as connected with the highest verb, *Bach* may be understood as the agens of *zingen*. (A pragmatic difficulty or a constraint of reality prevents us to make sense of this reading, since it seems impossible to hear loudly.) In (16)c, the constituent *Mariet* may not be understood as the agens of *zingen*; the sentence rather means that somebody is singing the name *Mariet*. In very much the same way we have to interpret *Bach* as the agens of *zingen* in (16)d.

Because the case agens is missing in (16)b, it becomes unclear to which of both syntactic levels the constituents *al dagenlang* and *luidkeels* should be considered to belong. The border is totally transparant. If the agens marks the beginning of the second set of constituents (according to (15)), the absence of that case will leave an open construction. The consequence is an ambiguity. We should interpret the sentence in different ways, putting the borderline as is indicated in (17):

(17) a. Peter heeft horen / al dagenlang luidkeels Bach zingen.
b. Peter heeft al dagenlang horen / luidkeels Bach zingen.
c. Peter heeft al dagenlang luidkeels horen / Bach zingen.

These interpretations are correct under the hypothesis only that *Bach* is to be interpreted as an objective. If we indicate an omitted agens as X, (17) has to be read as (18):

(18) a. Peter heeft horen / X al dagenlang luidkeels Bach zingen.
b. Peter heeft al dagenlang horen / X luidkeels Bach zingen.
c. Peter heeft al dagenlang luidkeels horen / X Bach zingen.

Since the reading with *Bach* as an objective is not necessary, the following reading has to be added to the three already mentioned:

(19) Peter heeft al dagenlang luidkeels horen / Bach (agens) zingen.

This means that a semantic interpreter should produce four readings of sentence (16)b. I do not touch upon the problem in the world, that *loudly* cannot be connected with *hearing*[34].

In it's present state, CASUS is not equiped for processing the transparant part of a surface structure with raising phenomena according to all possible readings. The algorithm operates under the assumption that all operators of the mixed domain belong to the lower level.

**The implementation**

As regards the implementation, I will speak of 1. modifications, needed in the subroutine 'Applicable structure'; 2. insertion of PRO constituents into S-complements; 3. semantic interpretation of PRO constituents in S-complements.

As will be dealt with in section 3.2.1.11, Testing a case frame, we use a rather severe way of testing the applicability of a certain case frame: as soon as a certain case candidate, which is not a possible operator, does not meet the claims of the case function currently tested, the conclusion is drawn that the frame as a whole does not apply. This severity is needed because of the great number of tests that is performed in constructions that show moving; cfr. section 3.2.1.8 about the sequence of the case candidates. However, in constructions that show mixing of constituents of several syntactic levels, this severe rule cannot be followed, since a raised NC preceeds the W2 construction (the S-complement) where it comes from and which itself is a case candidate in relation to the higher S. Look at the following instance:

(20) Patrick hoorde Lucie [ t Bach zingen.

where the candidates on the highest level are *Patrick*, *Lucie* and the S-complement. In this case, characterized by the fact that *hoorde* is a semi-auxiliary, we have to skip a constituent like *Lucie*, in order to find the correct objective more to the right. In this respect, the function 'Applicable structure' has been modified as to be capable of finding the case candidates of the highest verb.

In more detail, the algorithm has the following structure. The case functions of the verb that causes raising, i.e. a socalled semi-auxiliary, are tested in the basic sequence, according to (1) of section 3.2.1.8. With respect to (20) the first function to be tested will be the dative. If the sequence *Patrick*, *Lucie*, W2 is considered, the test will concern *Patrick*, which will be accepted. Then the function objective will follow. In connection with the verb *horen* (to hear), an

NC is not to be rejected beforehand, since *Lucie* seems to be acceptable, except, of course, in a construction with an S-complement. In that environment the constituent *Lucie* has to be considered as raised and to be skipped consequently. It is one of the constituents that should be lowered. The test of the function objective is repeated until a W2 is met. When no more functions are left, the function 'Applicable structure' makes sure that case candidates have been assigned to all semantic functions. If this seems to be the case, all remaining constituents are put apart, in order to wait for a possible assignment when the next level verb will be considered. The function returns successfully and the semantic interpretation of the verb is executed, i.e. the case carriers are attached to the verb node.

Before the test of the case frame of the next level verb will be performed, or, to speak generally, in every situation that a test has to be started, the set of lowered constituents is added at the left side of the set of constituents (possibly zero) that are already present at the syntactic level concerned. In the case of (20), the constituents *Lucie* and *Bach* will be added to the empty set already present at the level of *zingen* (to sing). Refer to section 3.2.1. to see how that information was organized.

Still another operation will have to be performed before the interpretation of the verb of the complement may start, viz. the occasional insertion of a PRO. If the verb of the preceeding level is of the type SUC or IOC (subject control or indirect object control; cfr. (1) above), a PRO has to be inserted anyway. If the verb is of the type RTO or RTS (raising to object or raising to subject), no PRO will be needed according to the theory discussed at the beginning of the present section. Sentence (20) receives the following interpretations:

(21) I.

```
                    SE
  __________________|________
 |   NC DAT            W2 OBJ
 |     |           _______|______
 |     |          |  NC AGE NC OBJ
 |     |          |     |      |
HOOR PATRICK ZING  LUCIE   BACH
```

ii.

```
                    SE
  __________________|_______
 |   NC DAT            W2 OBJ
 |     |           ______|_______
 |     |          |  NC AGE  NC OBJ
 |     |          |     |       |
HOOR  LUCIE ZING   BACH   PATRICK
```

```
iii.               SE
     ______________|______
     | NC DAT        W2 OBJ
     |    |      ______|______
     |    |     |  NC AGE NC OBJ
     |    |     |     |      |
   HOOR LUCIE ZING PATRICK  BACH
```

As will be clear, these results are not only due to the theory about raising but partly also to that of WH-movement and topicalization. Note that in the complement both *Patrick* and *Bach* may be considered as agens and objective, if topicalization of *Patrick* is hypothesized and if the lexicon ignores traditional composers. This remark will make clear that sentence (22):

(22) Patrick schijnt Lucie te horen zingen

will have to be detected as ambiguous. Apart from topicalization possible readings are:

(23) Patrick-i schijnt [ t-i Lucie-j te horen [ t-j zingen
Patrick-i schijnt [ t-i Lucie-j te horen [ PRO t-j zingen

This means that a complement like

(24) [ Lucie zingen

will have to be tested twice: once under the hypothesis that it has a raised agens and no objective and once that it has a PRO agens and a raised objective. Consequently, sentence (22) should receive the following interpretations:

```
(25) I.                 SE
        ________________|__
        |                W2 OBJ
        |      ____________|_______
        |     |   NC DAT        W2 OBJ
        |     |      |      ______|______
        |     |      |     |  NC AGE NC OBJ
        |     |      |     |     |      |
     SCHIJN HOOR PATRICK ZING   PRO   LUCIE
```

```
     ii.              SE
        ______________|___
        |              W2 OBJ
        |      __________|______
        |     |   NC DAT     W2 OBJ
        |     |      |      ___|___
        |     |      |     |  NC AGE
        |     |      |     |     |
     SCHIJN HOOR PATRICK ZING  LUCIE
```

iii.

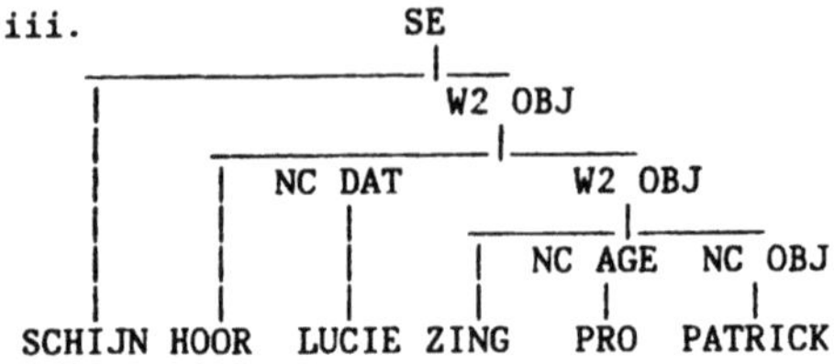
SE
W2 OBJ
NC DAT
W2 OBJ
NC AGE
NC OBJ
SCHIJN HOOR LUCIE ZING PRO PATRICK

iv.

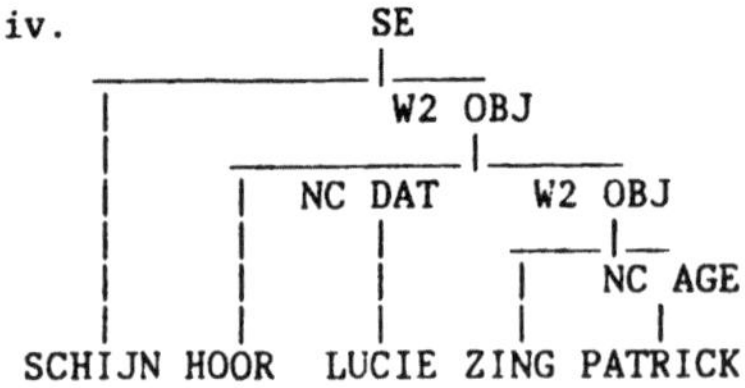
SE
W2 OBJ
NC DAT
W2 OBJ
NC AGE
SCHIJN HOOR LUCIE ZING PATRICK

### 3.2.1.10 AMBIGUITY AND SEMANTIC EQUIVALENCE

As one of the last subjects of this chapter about the translation of AMAZON-structures into SELANCA-expressions, let us look to the question of the ambiguities of the latter or rather to the way SELANCA-expressions are related with AMAZON-structures and with each other. For that matter, consider first figure (1):

(1)

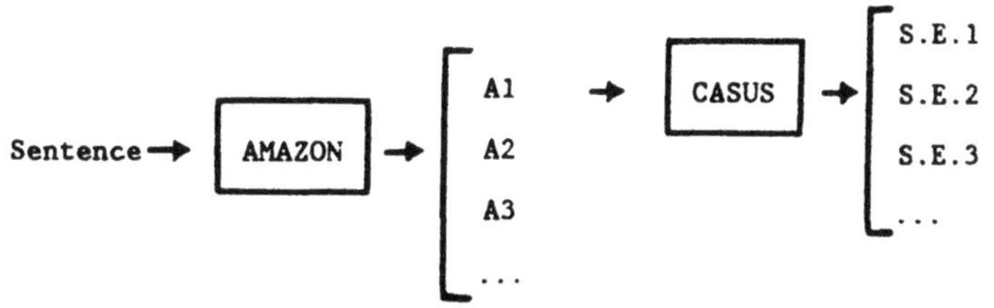


This figure (1) indicates, that AMAZON assigns possibly more than one syntactic structure to an input sentence. To one or more AMAZON interpretations (A1, A2, etc.) a set of SELANCA representations (S.E.1, S.E.2, etc.) may be assigned by CASUS. All SELANCA representations of an AMAZON structure Ai are claimed to reflect different and correct meanings of the input sentence. With respect to an input sentence S however may hold: the SELANCA representation S.E.i of AMAZON structure Aj of S is identical with SELANCA representation S.E.k of AMAZON structure Al of S. With respect to the sentences S-n and S-m may hold: the SELANCA representation S.E.i of AMAZON structure Ak of S-n is identical with the SELANCA representation S.E.j of AMAZON structure Al of S-m. Look at the sentences (2):

(2) a. Jan dacht ik dat Piet een boek gaf.
   (John thought I that Peter a book gave)
   b. Piet dacht ik dat Jan een boek gaf.

In the following schemes the AMAZON structures and the SELANCA representations are shown. In (3) the AMAZON-structure is given of (2)a. The figures (4) and (5) show it's SELANCA-representations. Sentence (2)a appears to be ambiguous since both *Jan* and *Piet* may be interpreted as both dative and agentive. The sentence (2)b with topicalization of *Piet* is shown with it's AMAZON structure in (6), and it's SELANCA representations in (7) and (8). Comparison with the set (3-4-5) shows that both sentences (2)a and (2)b get the same pair of semantic interpretations: (4) and (8) and (5) and (7) are identical.

(3)

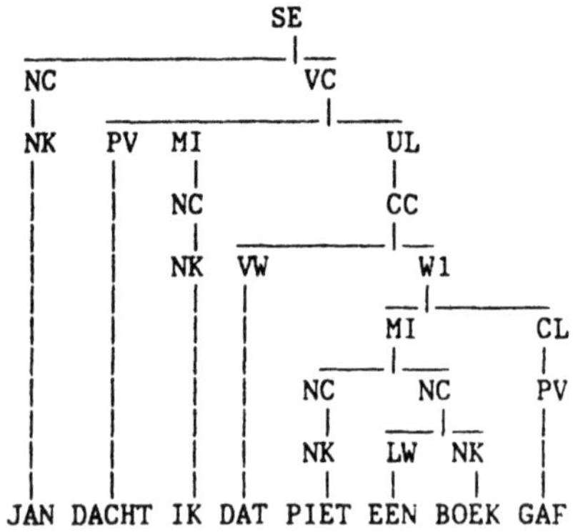
SE
NC VC
NK PV MI UL
NC CC
NK VW W1
MI CL
NC NC PV
NK LW NK
JAN DACHT IK DAT PIET EEN BOEK GAF

(4)

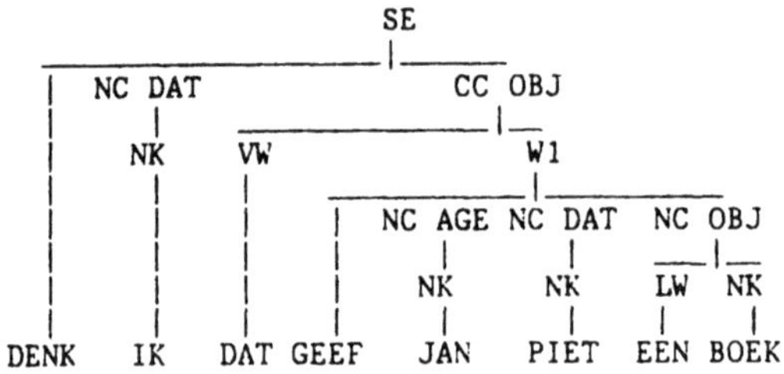
SE
NC DAT CC OBJ
NK VW W1
NC AGE NC DAT NC OBJ
NK NK LW NK
DENK IK DAT GEEF JAN PIET EEN BOEK

(5)

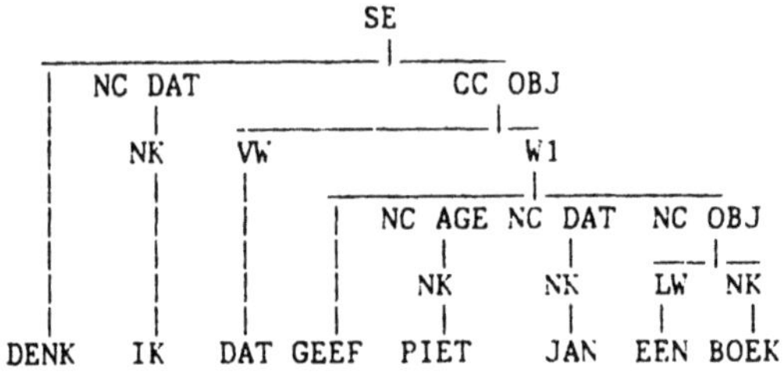
SE
NC DAT CC OBJ
NK VW W1
NC AGE NC DAT NC OBJ
NK NK LW NK
DENK IK DAT GEEF PIET JAN EEN BOEK

(6)

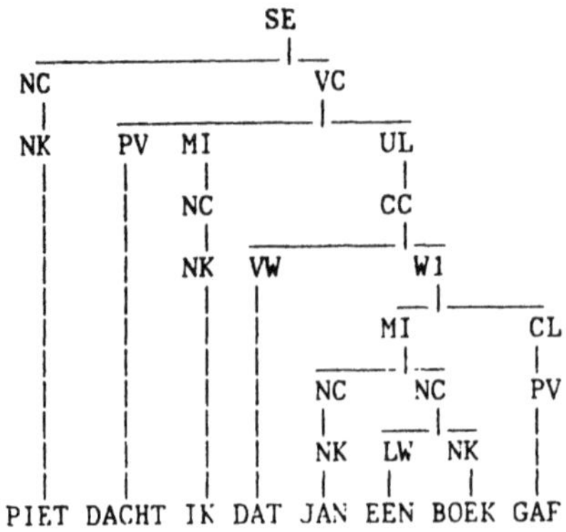
SE
NC VC
NK PV MI UL
NC CC
NK VW W1
MI CL
NC NC PV
NK LW NK
PIET DACHT IK DAT JAN EEN BOEK GAF

This means that the choice of the actual constituent to be moved by topicalization as such does not cause a semantic difference.

(7)

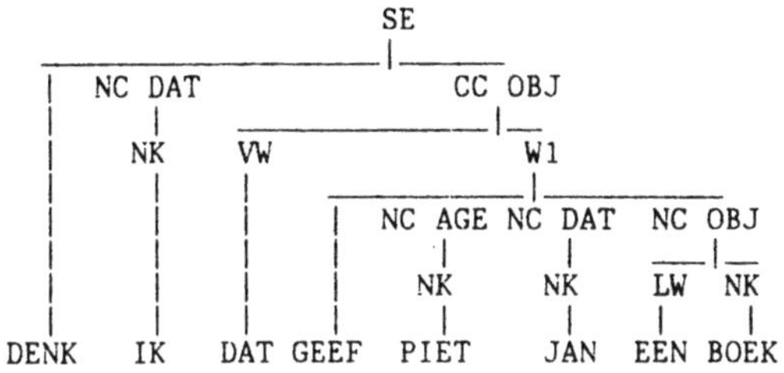


(8)

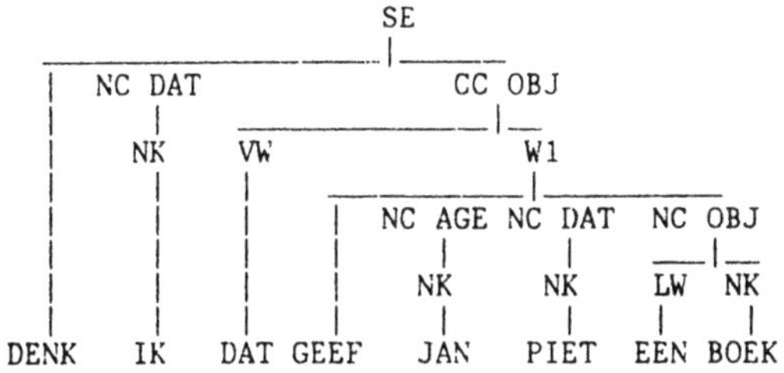


The meaning relations between the following sentences are not caused by topicalization.

(9) a. Ik zag de man met mijn verrekijker meestal.
(I saw the man with my telescope mostly)
b. Ik zag de man meestal met mijn verrekijker.

AMAZON and CASUS assign to (9)a and (9)b the following structures:

(10)

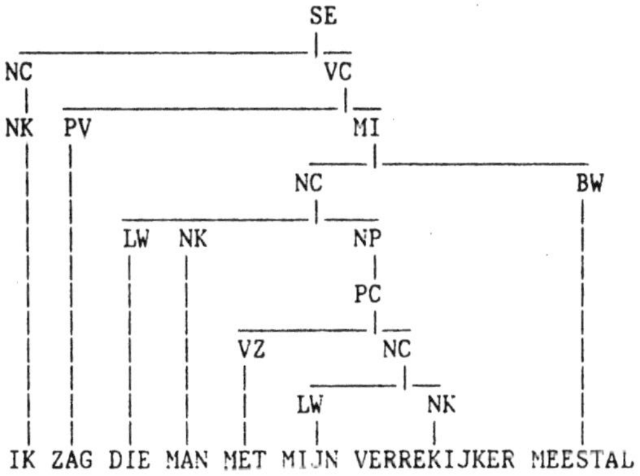

(11)

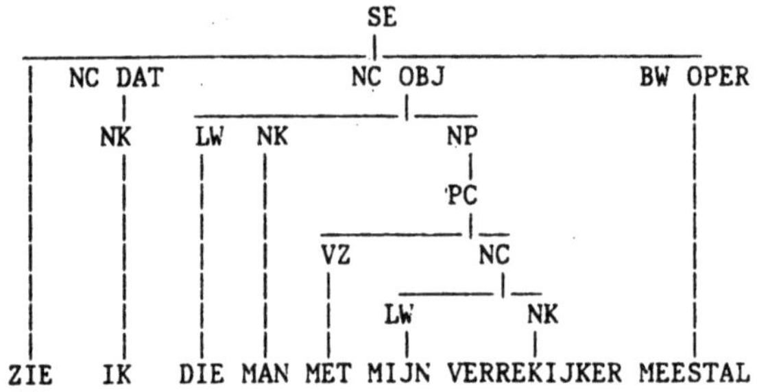
SE
NC DAT
NC OBJ
BW OPER
NK
LW
NK
NP
PC
VZ
NC
LW
NK
ZIE IK DIE MAN MET MIJN VERREKIJKER MEESTAL

(12)

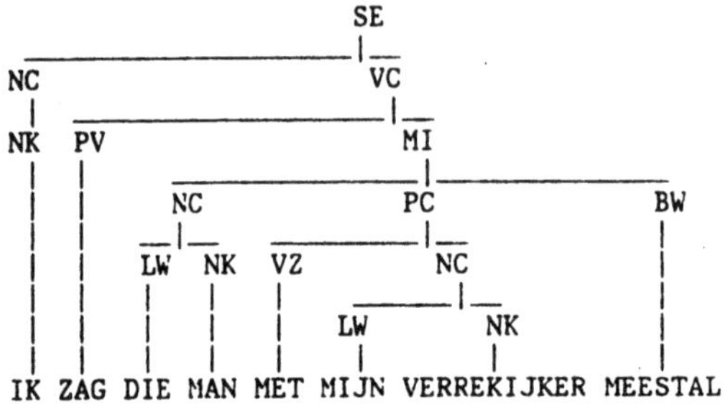
SE
NC
VC
NK
PV
MI
NC
PC
BW
LW
NK
VZ
NC
LW
NK
IK ZAG DIE MAN MET MIJN VERREKIJKER MEESTAL

(13)

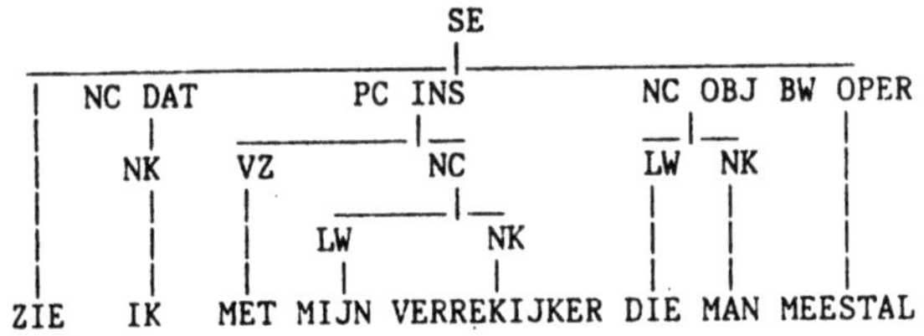
SE
NC DAT
PC INS
NC OBJ
BW OPER
NK
VZ
NC
LW
NK
LW
NK
ZIE IK MET MIJN VERREKIJKER DIE MAN MEESTAL

(14)

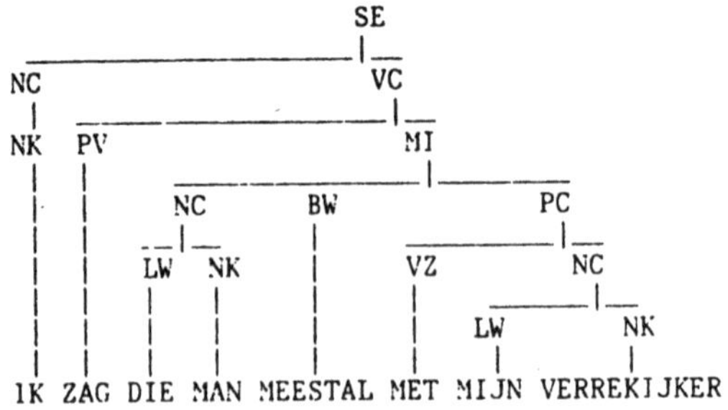
SE
NC
VC
NK
PV
MI
NC
BW
PC
LW
NK
VZ
NC
LW
NK
IK ZAG DIE MAN MEESTAL MET MIJN VERREKIJKER

(15)

```
                              SE
 _____________________________|_______________________
|  NC DAT          PC INS            NC OBJ BW OPER
|     |     ______________|__        __|__          |
|    NK    VZ             NC         LW   NK        |
|     |     |      _______|__         |    |        |
|     |     |   LW           NK       |    |        |
|     |     |    |            |       |    |        |
ZIE   IK   MET MIJN VERREKIJKER DIE MAN MEESTAL
```

(16)

```
                            SE
 ___________________________|__
NC                            VC
 |    ________________________|___________
NK  PV           MI                      UL
 |   |        ____|____                   |
 |   |       NC       BW                  PC
 |   |      _|__       |       ___________|__
 |   |     LW   NK     |      VZ           NC
 |   |      |    |     |       |     ______|__
 |   |      |    |     |       |   LW        NK
 |   |      |    |     |       |    |         |
IK ZAG DIE MAN MEESTAL MET MIJN VERREKIJKER
```

(17)

```
                              SE
 _____________________________|_______________________
|  NC DAT          PC INS            NC OBJ BW OPER
|     |     ______________|__        __|__          |
|    NK    VZ             NC         LW   NK        |
|     |     |      _______|__         |    |        |
|     |     |   LW           NK       |    |        |
|     |     |    |            |       |    |        |
ZIE   IK   MET MIJN VERREKIJKER DIE MAN MEESTAL
```

Here we find two different input sentences, which receive two different AMAZON structures each; see (10) and (12) for the first sentence (9)a and (14) and (18) for the second sentence (9)b. Every separate AMAZON structure is mapped into one SELANCA representation by CASUS. See the trees (11), (13), (15) and (17) for these four structures respectively. Note that the trees (13), (15) and (17) are identical. The semantic relations between the sentences and structures concerned can be schematized as follows:

(18)

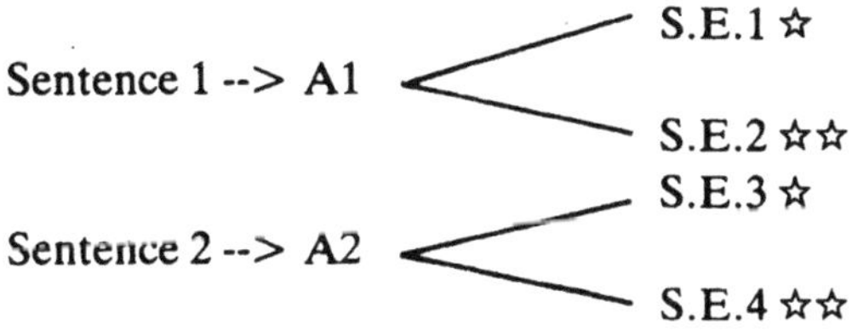

This figure, again, puts the question about ambiguity in a compelling way. In linguistic literature, this term often is used inexplicitly. The term ambiguity as related to formal systems has to be interpreted as follows: if an element e' of a formal system s' is, according to some interpreting rules, to be associated with a set of elements e''1...e''n (n > 1) of a formal system s'', the element e' is called ambiguous in the relation s' - s''. Semantic equivalence or synonymy is exactly the opposite phenomenon and has also meaning only as a relation between elements of two formal systems: if a set of elements e''1...e''n (n > 1) of a formal system s'' is, according to a set of interpreting rules, to be associated with only one element e' of a formal system s', the elements e''1...e''n are called semantically equivalent in the relation s'' - s'. Neither ambiguity nor synonymy can be self-evident. Saying that A and B are synonymous, one is always implicitly referring to a relation between two systems as indicated. Figure (18) might be considered to display meaning relations between three languages: the language of the 'Sentences', the language A and the language S.E. Let us confine ourselves to A and S.E. for convenience. Then we establish a twofold ambiguity of A1 in the relation A - S.E. and the same holds for A2. No special remarks have to be made about A3 through A6, none of these being ambiguous in the relation A - S.E. Considered from the language S.E., a semantic equivalence has to be established between S.E.1 and S.E.2 and between S.E.3 and S.E.4, both in the relation S.E. - A. Nothing has to be said about S.E.5 through S.E.8 in this respect. As soon as the language of 'Sentences' (i.e. Dutch) is considered, things are going to change, since we can establish ambiguities and semantic equivalences in the relation Dutch - A: both sentence 3 end sentence 4 are twofold ambiguous, and both A3 plus A4 and A5 plus A6 are semantically equivalent pairs. For a correct interpretation of the developed model we are describing, no separate meaning should be assigned to sentences of A, since what we are really doing is: expressing the meaning of sentences of Dutch via a two step analyzing translation into S.E. Therefore, we should neglect the language A and establish the twofold ambiguity of the sentences 1 through 4 in the relation Dutch - S.E.[35]

The next question is about the theoretical status of the identities, indicated by the asterisks in (18). It is evident, that the problem is caused by the fact that the semantic analyzer neglects certain sentence features that originate in moving transformations or, formulated more safely, that are to be reduced to differences in place or sequence. The sentences (2)a and (2)b differ by the choice of the constituent that is topicalized; the sentences (9)a and (9)b differ in the sequence of the sentence parts. It may be concluded that these differences do not cause semantic differences according to our opinion. When a number of Dutch sentences are interpreted which differ from each other in the choice of the sentence part only which is topicalized, al these sentences will be considered semantically equivalent in the relation Dutch - Selanca (S.E.). WH-movement does not differ from topicalization in this respect; it only differs in that it embodies an obligatory topicalization, which fact is of no relevance for the meaning representation as such.

This dicussion about ambiguity of sentences and semantic equivalences is of principal importance for the meaning problem in general. The question may be raised as to whether it is correct indeed to state that there are syntactic phenomena which need not be accounted for semantically. The question is not typical for our approach, as it is raised also within Montague grammar[36]. The phenomena that are neglected in the Selanca expressions are mainly identical with what Jackendoff [1972] calls *Focus*; matters of *presupposition*, introduced by this author in the same context, stay out of discussion here. I consider focus as a special subject, just as Jackendoff does, which should be dealt with on a level of interpretation that may follow long behind the *functional* level that mainly is accounted for within my model. Different sequences as occurred in (9) are looked upon as being of the same semantic kind principally.

### 3.2.1.11 TESTING A CASE FRAME

In this last section we will see in detail how the algorithm is built which decides the applicability of a certain case frame in relation to a certain set of case candidates, put in a certain order according to the actual hypothesis about their generation. What is being explained is mainly the content of the subroutine 'Applicable Structure'. It may be clear on the basis of the foregoing sections, that we need not worry on this level of analysis about the other possible reconstructions of the original sequence of the case candidates, nor about other possibly applicable case frames, nor about occasional other problems concerning the semantic interpretation of the semantic kernel at hand. For convenience, I make use of a diagram to support the explanation.

```
(1)  1. Next Case Function.
     2. Next Case Candidate.
                        Is this
                        Case candidate acceptable
                        for this case function? -------------------------- No --> Fail
                                    |
                                   Yes
                                    |
                        Is this the case function
                        ATTRIBUTE ? -----------------------------------No --> 3.
                                    |
                                   Yes
                                    |
                        Build the structure wanted
                        for this case candidate (Bound ATT).
                                    |
     3.                 Allocate candidate for this case.
                        Release the verb's case claim.
                                    |
                        Is this the case function
                        ATTRIBUTE ? -----------------------------------No --> 1.
                                    |
                                   Yes
                                    |
                        Is there a case candidate with the
                        form of an attribute? -------------------------No --> 1.
                                    |
                                   Yes
                                    |
                        Does this verb claim an ATT ? -----------------No --> 4.
                                    |
```

```
                    Yes
                     |
    Has one of the following case
    candidates an attribute form ? -------------------No --> 1.
                     |
                    Yes
                     |
4.  Build a structure wanted for the
    next case candidate. (Free ATT)
                     |
                     ------------------------------------------ --> 1.
```

As the figure suggests, the algorithm iterates over the different case functions and, on a lower level, over the case candidates. The first iteration is driven by a complete set of case names, some of which are names of functions, claimed by the main verb concerned at the moment. Others are not and will be skipped. Apart from administrative details, the next test concerns the acceptability of the case candidate for the case function considered. The test is performed by the subroutine 'Acceptable cand for case' (see section 2 of the appendix). If the test fails, the iteration stops and the function 'Applicable structure' itself fails. In section 3.2.1.8 I dealt with the question why this conclusion can be drawn already in this early instance. If the case function tested just now is the ATT(ribute), a datastructure is built which is adequate for this function.

I have to make a note concerning this point. As the rest of the algorithm described will show, the succeeding of the subroutine 'Acceptable cand for case' with the function ATT will always concern a bound attribute, i.e. an attribute which is subcategorized by the main verb considered. This means, that the case candidate in question must be interpreted as a case function in connection with the main verb and that a raised constituent from the small clause functions as an object in relation to this attribute. The reader should refer to section 3.2.1.7 Attributes for details. The building of the structure needed now has to imply the construction of a tree for a semantic kernel of type A with some other constituent (one of the case candidates) as it's object. The object role in connection with the attribute must be played by the constituent that has been detected as a provisional pseudo-object in relation to the verb of the construction. Again, I must refer to the section dealing with the Attributes for details on this point. Afterwards (point 3), the case candidate is allocated as the case carrier of the semantic function considered.

At this point it has to be established whether the next case candidate, immediately following the one that has been allocated just now, has the form of an attribute. If this is not the case, the iteration on the first level has to be continued. If it is the case and if the verb considered claims an ATT as an argument, the next case candidate may play that role. If, however, some of the case candidates to follow after the next one has an attribute form too, the attribute that was found on the next place can impossibly be the bound ATT of the verb, since this has to appear as the last candidate in the set. This in turn means, that the attribute that follows immediately has another function: it will have to be interpreted as a free attribute in connection with the case candidate that has been allocated just now. (If the last function to which a case candidate was assigned was itself an ATT, the construction will have to be marked ungrammatical and the test of the applicability as a whole will fail. Success leads to the building of a structure as wanted for the situation met.) The next case candidate is interpreted as an attribute function in connection with the semantic kernel N of 'this' case candidate, so this will always be a free attribute. Afterwards, the iteration of level 1 is continued.

It should be noticed that this explanation and the attention paid to the algorithm have a good reason. It is important to see how the decisions about case functions on different levels of semantic kernels interfere. Look at a sentence like (2)

(2) Ik vind muziek lelijk
(I find music ugly)

The sentence consists of four words which represent four semantic kernels. According to the AMAZON surface structure, the V *vind* is the main centre, and the three other constituents have a problematic function as opposed to each other and in relation to the verb: every N may function as an argument of the verb or as an argument of the A *lelijk*. The A may function as an argument of the V or as an argument of every N separately. It would be possible to organize the semantic interpreting algorithm in the following way: 1. collect all sentence parts that are semantic kernels; 2. test successively all semantic kernels in all possible interpretations, i.e. with every possible set of arguments. With respect to the example sentence (2) this would yield the following tests:

(3) V vind ( N(ik) N(muziek A(lelijk)))
V vind ( N(ik A(lelijk)) N(muziek))
V vind ( N(ik) A(lelijk N(muziek)))
V vind ( N(muziek) A(lelijk N(ik)))
V vind ( N(ik) N(muziek) A(lelijk))

The syntax AMAZON together with the theory implied in CASUS will have to decide about the acceptability of the different interpretations suggested in (3). It has to be noticed, that in (3) the V (vind) never may be considered as an argument of *ik*, *muziek* or *lelijk*. This is entailed by the syntactic theory of AMAZON, which, apart from raising phenomena by which the order of the constituents may be disturbed, indicates what part has to be considered as the semantic kernel on a certain level. Within the present context, the problem is whether the A is an argument of an N or of a V or the other way round. A theory about this is implied in 'Applicable structure', according to which an A may be considered as an argument of a V that has been marked therefore in the lexicon, or of an N.

The semantic interpretation as it operates in CASUS deals with the different main verbs of a sentence successively and, while processing the environment of a certain verb, also handles the occasional A and N kernels. The algorithm illustrated in (1) clearly shows this. (It has to be noted that, as has been mentioned earlier, the interpretation of the semantic kernel N has hardly started yet.) It would be possible and perhaps wanted, to deal with semantic kernels of different type in the same way as is done with the V. Just as CASUS performs general routines to adequately handle the verb raising and the raising of constituents from an S-complement to a higher construction, it might also perform such procedures for raising out of small clauses. This however would considerably complicate the semantic interpretation, since it seems to be impossible to let those general procedures be constrained by lexical features of certain lexical items as is done with verb raising. This may be detected on the basis of lexical categorial information and of certain sequences of verbs in a Cl(uster). That information leads deterministically to the conclusion about verb raising. No such conclusion is possible with respect to the N's and the A's of a sentence.

The building of the adequate structures for bound and free attributes, as meant in certain parts of (1), concerns the following. A free attribute is assigned as a semantic argument to the N to which it belongs. In fact this means a kind of lowering: the constituent is taken away from between the case candidates and is connected as a son to the N of the NC concerned. In very much the same way the operation is performed with respect to a bound attribute, although in this case the NC is lowered and assigned as a son to the attribute.

The attaching of constituents as sons of other constituents of the sentence (a V, N or A), is the very heart of the semantic interpretation that is performed. According to the description of SELANCA expressions in (9) of section 3.1, the attaching concerns not only the constituent that occurs in the set of case candidates but also it's semantic function. This aspect of the interpretation is provided for by the subroutine 'Acceptable cand for case', about which some remarks still have to be made. This subroutine, called for every case candidate that has to be judged, operates with information about the case frame and about all lexical and syntactic features of the case candidate under consideration. The first thing to be done in the subroutine is to verify whether the candidate has all internal features that are claimed by the verb's lexical specifications. This regards the lexical category and a set of semantic features. The work is performed by the subroutine called 'All case claims met', which in turn calls the function 'Test claims'. In some instances the test has to take into account the voice of the sentence: in case of depassivization, a constituent with accusative features will be acceptable as an agentive, etc. Some morphological features like singular and plural are also considered. After this test, some other things are examined, depending on the question which case function precisely is concerned. With respect to a dative e.g. it matters whether an Agentive function has been assigned to some constituent earlier; if that is not the case, the Dative may not be assigned to a preposition phrase. Quite a lot of other considerations of rather low level are built into the function, which would take some space to be fully characterized. I will skip them, however, referring to section 3 of the appendix for a full description.

If the highest iteration of (1) ends, the subroutine continues by evaluating it's own results. It checkes whether to all case candidates functions have been assigned. If one or more are left, the subroutine tries to assign to them operator functions. The process continues, whatever may be the result of this, with a test whether perhaps an obliged case function did not get a case candidate. If that is the case, a search is undertaken whether to an optional case function a case candidate has been assigned, which might be acceptable in the role of the unfulfilled obliged function. The positive end of the process is, that to all obliged cases candidates have been assigned and that no one candidate is left without a semantic role.

In the foregoing discussion, no attention has been paid to special features of the algorithm, needed to correctly process constructions with verb raising. For details about that the reader should refer to section 3.2.1.9.

### 3.2.2 DETAILS OF THE IMPLEMENTATION

This section 3.2.2 deals with subjects that are to be characterized as formal and technical rather than linguistic, although the latter will not be totally absent. The information is intended to enable the reader to get a more precise idea about the distance or rather the absence of distance between the formalism and the theory.

#### 3.2.2.1 THE LEXICAL FEATURES

We will first make some remarks about the set of semantic lexical features that are used by CASUS.

Features of nouns and pronouns.

In the lexicon a noun is marked for the following features:

(1) 1. human
2. animate
3. living
4. concrete
5. time
6. place
7. gender
8. sex
9. script
10. count
11. audible

The features for time and place share one marking field together, so that only ten places are used. A pronoun is marked for the features:

(2) 1. singular
2. human
3. 1st person
4. nominative
5. genitive
6. accusative
7. dative
8. sex

Again here different features share one and the same place, viz. 4 and 5 and 6 and 7; only 6 places are used. (For some examples of lexical entries, see section 4 of the appendix.) The features are defined in a non redundant way. Redundancy rules are incorporated in CASUS. Possible feature values in the lexicon are "1", "2", "0" and empty. The meaning of these values is different for different features. During execution the lexical feature values are translated in such a way that the following set of binary features is yielded:

| | | |
|---|---|---|
| (3) | 1. human | HUM |
| | 2. animate | ANI |
| | 3. living | LIV |
| | 4. abstract | ABS |
| | 5. concrete | CCR |
| | 6. local | LOC |
| | 7. temporal | TEM |
| | 8. male or female | MOF |
| | 9. neuter | NEU |
| | 10. male | MAL |
| | 11. female | FEM |
| | 12. count | CNT |
| | 13. script | SCR |
| | 14. audible | AUD |
| | 15. singular | SIN |
| | 16. plural | PLU |
| | 17. singular or plural | SOP |
| | 18. not human | NOT.HUM |
| | 19. 1st person | PE1 |
| | 20. 2nd person | PE2 |
| | 21. 3rd person | PE3 |
| | 22. genitive | GEN |
| | 23. accusative | ACC |
| | 24. dative | DAT |
| | 25. nominative | NOM |

With respect to these, CASUS contains the following redundancy rules:

| | | | | |
|---|---|---|---|---|
| (4) | PRONOUN: | +NEU | : | +CCR , +ABS . |
| | | −NEU | : | +HUM , +ANI , +LIV , +CCR , +CNT ,+AUD . |
| | NOUN: | | : | +ACC , +DAT , +NOM , +PE3 . |
| | | +HUM | : | +ANI , +LIV . |
| | | +ANI | : | +LIV . |
| | | +LIV | : | +CCR . |

Features for verbs: case frames.

Semantic subclasses of verbs in our theory are, according to the subcategorization rules: +agentive , +objective; +agentive , +dative , +objective, etc. A verb like *denken* (to think) is lexically marked:

(5) DAT(),OBJ(+ABS),*

The asterisk is the delimiter for this case frame. It is the subdivision on the dollarsign level of the structure indicated in figure (1) of section 3.2.2.2. A verb may have more than one case frame. In this notation DAT() means the case dative in the sense of Fillmore [1968] and, likewise, OBJ() means the case objective. The features claimed for a case candidate are indicated between parentheses. Empty parentheses indicate default feature values for the constituent that plays the role in question, for which CASUS uses redundancy rules to specify them. The redundancy rules that predict feature values of case candidates are:

| | | | |
|---|---|---|---|
| (6) | AGE() | : | +ANI/NP . |
| | OBJ() | : | /NP . |
| | OBJ(+ABS) | : | +ACC/NP ; /CC/DAT ; /CC/OF ; /W2 ; /W1 . |
| | DAT() | : | +ANI . |
| | INS() | : | +CCR/PP/MET . |
| | LOK() | : | +LOK . |
| | ATT() | : | /AJ . |

The specification of a value configuration may be given with respect to three aspects: 1) a number of semantic features, 2) the syntactic form (syntactic label) and 3) the actual preposition or conjunction with which the constituent has to start. The redundancy rule for +ABS objective specifies that it should be an NC in accusative form, a conjunction construction starting with *dat* (that) or *of* (whether), a W2 (-tense S with an inifinitive) or a W1 (+tense S).

### 3.2.2.2 THE FORM OF THE LEXICON

The lexicon that is used by CASUS has two forms, one outside the computer program and one during the execution. Both are of course intimately connected. Let us first look at the structure of a lexical item while residing on disc.

(1) lexical item : base word form , $ ,
word category , $ ,
word type , $ ,
features , $ ,
variants , $@ .

The lexical item is defined as a string consisting of substrings separated by special characters (dollar signs). Another special character, the at sign (@), marks the end of the item. The base word form is an arbitrary chosen morphological form, one of the word's alternates. A verb's base form is the first person singular present tense, that of a noun is the singular form, that of an adjective is the uninflected form. The word's category is one of this series: noun, pronoun, verb, adjective, adverb, adverbial part of a separable verb, article, preposition and conjunction. A symbol for the word's type is a means for a generalization on a lower level than the word's category. With respect to verbs, for instance, it is possible to speak of "indirect object control", "subject control", "modal auxiliary" etc. A symbol for the word's type is used in connection with both nouns and verbs.

The FEATURES of a lexical item are of different type according to the different word categories. The differences between verbs and nouns are of special importance. We wil return to this subject instantly.

The VARIANTS part of a lexical item contains the different forms of the word in question. As we are mainly interested in syntax, we did not try to build sophisticated morphological routines for CASUS. As a matter of fact, AMAZON has some morphological knowledge and at present some effort is made to optimize the morphological cooperation between AMAZON and CASUS. The cooperation, however, is not optimal as yet. That is why inflectional forms are defined in the lexicon in an ad hoc way. With respect to a verb the VARIANTS contain: the second and third person singular present time, the first person plural present time, the infinitive, thc present participle, the form of the past tense singular, the past tense plural and the past participle. See for some examples section 4 of the appendix.

According to (1) the form of a lexical item during execution is:

(2) WORD
CATEGORY
TYPE
FEATURES
VARIANTS

Different types of FEATURE values are given for nouns, verbs, adjectives and adverbs. All but the verb's have string values. Figure (3) shows the datastructure of the verbal FEATURES field during execution of the program.

(3)

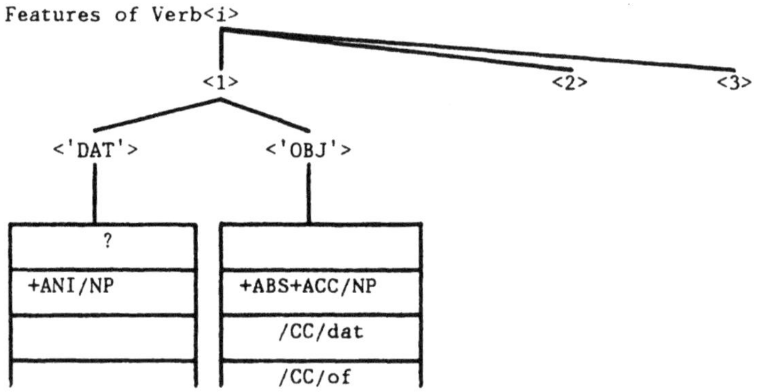


The data object at it's highest level is an array. Every element of the array is a SNOBOL table, the elements of which are pointed at with a three character literal (mnemonics for the case in question). Every element of such a table is, again, an array. The first element of these arrays may contain a question mark, indicating that the case in question is optional. The second and following elements contain three place values for semantic feature, syntactic form and starting word respectively, which represent a set of claims for the features of the constituent, tested for the case function. One of the sets (the second, or the third etc.) should be met for the positive conclusion that the observed constituent is acceptable for the case function under consideration. The test is performed by the subroutine 'All case claims met' that contains an iterative call of the function 'Test claims'. See for details section 2 of the appendix.

### 3.2.2.3 THE TREE STRUCTURE

The interpreting algorithm, defined in the computer program CASUS is mainly a set of subroutines which operate on a tree structure of a certain type. Nothing but the nodes of this tree structure and their relations is the data for the algorithm. This algorithm embodies the semantic interpreting theory that is defined as a complex function of a certain type. The structure of the algorithm has been explained throughout this study and will be dealt with in still more detail in the appendix. In this section the structure of the data will be characterized by describing the information organization in the nodes of the tree structure.

The first part of the algorithm under CASUS reads an AMAZON sentence. As has been mentioned earlier, the sentence structure is a labeled bracketing, the labels having the form of a two character string. A recursive function 'Analyse' (see the appendix, section 2) decomposes the string and builds a tree structure in core. The nodes of the structure that is built have the form:

(1) FATHER
VALUE
WORD
LEX
ASPECT
WH
NUMBER
GENDER
PT

An object of this form is created by calling a SNOBOL data defining function. Afterwards values are assigned to the variables of the created node. The FATHER field gets as it's value a pointer to the node directly dominating this node. (Note by the way that by eventually deleting or changing this pointer value, the node pointed at is not affected at all, so it is easy to attach a node to another father, changing the tree structure as a whole).

The label of a certain opening bracket of the AMAZON structure is assigned as the value of the field VALUE. If the node is to be a leaf of the tree, the value of the variable WORD is the word met in the AMAZON structure. The variable LEX is used to bear a pointer to the lexical element with which the WORD has to be associated. The variable ASPECT is only used if the node refers to a verbal element of the sentence and, more precisely, if this verbal element is a main verb in connection with which one or more auxiliary verbs are used. During the processing of the sentence these auxiliaries will be detached from their original places and put aside on this variable of the main verb to which they are related.

The variable WH has to contain the pointer to the WH-constituent that has to be associated with a certain main verb of the sentence, according to the exposition of section 3.2.1.5. Note, that, in this case, the variable is only used if the node concerns a main verb. The variable is also used to carry referential information in case a PRO constituent is concerned.

The variable NUMBER contains a numeric value that is associated with the order of generation: all the nodes of the sentence get a sequence number as an easy means to identify them.

The variable GENDER is used to keep the conclusion of the investigation of a certain node's number and person in cases of agreement between subject and verb. It is only used when a possible subject of the sentence is concerned.

The variable PT is an array of pointers (maximally 10) to the sons of this node. In connection with these also, it should be noticed that changing the pointer value does not affect the objects pointed at, so it is easy to replace subtrees, as is needed for the semantic interpretation.

### 3.2.2.4 THE LINKS BETWEEN TREE AND LEXICON

In this section some remarks will be made about the way the lexical information is made available on the nodes of the tree structure. When a labeled bracketing is input and has been changed into a tree structure by the function 'Analyse', nothing more than syntactic labels and the words of the sentence constitute the information that is contained in the tree. The words together with the syntactic labels will be used to decide with which lexical items the nodes will have to be enriched semantically. The connection of the nodes with a certain lexical item is performed by the function 'Consult lexicon', which operates on every separate node, calling in turn the function 'Retrieve L.I'.

The items of the lexicon are ordered arbitrarily, just as they were found in the external dataset. For every node that is a leaf of the tree, the items of the lexicon are inspected sequentially, until a fitting item has been found. If none is present, the calling routine will fail and cause a skipping of the sentence. The reason is, that certain functions to be used during the semantic interpretation will yield unreliable results if the lexical information should be missing. A message about this will be sent to the user.

The way the decision is made whether a certain lexical item is to be connected with the word considered is little specific, so it need not be discussed in detail. The decision is based upon comparing the word with one of the variants of the lexical item (cfr. section 3.2.2.2).

If the lexical item matches, a copy of it is made, to which a pointer is set in the word's field 'Lex' (cfr. section 3.2.2.3). That a copy is needed rather than a simple pointer to the lexical item regarded is easily concluded from the fact, that the semantic features will have to be completed in certain cases. It may appear for instance that a noun has a plural form, which information should be present in the syntactic node and cannot be part of the lexicon.

### 3.2.2.5 POPPING THE LEXICAL INFORMATION

As figure (1) in section 3.2.1 shows, the reading of an input sentence and the consulting of the lexicon (section 3.2.2.4) is followed by the operation called 'Pop lexical information'. The present section deals with that operation.

In order to make a decision about the semantic function of a certain constituent, it's syntactic and semantic features will have to be tested. The semantic features will mainly be determined by the features of the construction's head, so to answer the question as to which semantic role can be played by a constituent, it will be needed to retrieve the features of the head. Since this testing process is repeated continuously during the semantic analysis, it seems preferable to bring the semantic information which is represented in the node of the head, to the top of the constituent once for all before the semantic interpretation starts. That operation is defined in the function 'Pop lexical information'.

Just like 'Consult lexicon', also 'Pop lexical information' is a recursive function, which treats all nodes of the tree structure, calling from every point the function 'Semantic kernel'. This function ensures that the top node of a constituent, to which no lexical item has been attached by 'Consult lexicon', is given a LEX structure (cfr. figure (1) of section 3.2.2.2), which is filled with information that is retrieved from the head by the function 'Find kernel' and, possibly, with some redundant feature specifications. Obviously, the function 'Find kernel' is of decisive importance.

'Find kernel' has only sense in relation with the assigning of a semantic function to a sentence constituent. That is why only nodes of a specific syntactic status will have to be considered. Since for instance a node with label UL never will be a member of the set of case candidates, the function 'Find kernel' need not operate on it. In figure (1) a survey is given of the nodes that should get semantic information from their heads. It is a simple paring of the syntactic labels of the top nodes and their heads.

| | | | |
|---|---|---|---|
| (1) | CC | with head VW (conjunction) | |
| | PC | ... | head of dominated node |
| | AV | ... | itself |
| | BW | ... | itself |
| | AJ | ... | AK (adjective) |
| | NC | ... | NK (noun or pronoun) |
| | W1 | ... | first part under MI |

| | | |
|---|---|---|
| W2 | ... | first part under MI |
| W3 | ... | first part under MI |
| W4 | ... | first part under MI |
| W5 | ... | first part under MI |

It should be noticed, that the retrieving of the semantic information as such is not decisive for the actual semantic interpretation of the constituent. It only satisfies the conditions for a certain constituent to be judged about it's semantic function.

This section gives only a global impression of things dealt with. Some details have been left aside.

# 4 Conclusion

The reader may now form an opinion about the automatic semantic interpretation of Dutch sentences as it is reported in this study. Most aspects of the system have been dealt with, some of them in great detail, so the description presented may be considered to be a sufficient basis for a justified judgement. Nevertheless, it seems to be not superfluous to complete the explanation by paying some attention to the shortcomings and lacks of the system in it's present state. If it may not be a specific task of the author to deal with that, it may prevent misunderstandings if he himself appears to see, almost as well as the reader, what should be improved and what should be added, to get an acceptable instrument for semantic interpretation, how pretentious it may seem to be altogether to suggest that an acceptable level could be reached with that.

Let us depart from establishing that the present system works fairly well. The parts of theory that have been implemented in it may be appreciated positively, because of both their correctness and the way they are working. That is a nice basis not to resign, but to continue the work and to look for improvements and extensions.

In trying to evaluate what has been attained, let us look at the main topics of our interpretation, viz. the three semantic kernels: V, N and A. It is quite clear that a great deal of our attention was paid to the V. Nevertheless, there are things to do also in connection with that. In the verbal structures, it is mainly the extraposition which is waiting for an interpretative theory. I think nobody will be surprised that the subject got little attention. Extraposition of constituents often concerns prepositional phrases, both subconstituents and constituents. Look at the examples of (1)

(1) Paul had van Marie gehouden.
    Paul had gehouden van Marie.
    (Paul had loved Mary)
    Paul had de hand van Marie gekust.
    Paul had de hand gekust van Marie.
    (Paul had kissed Mary's hand)

At a first glance, it does not seem too difficult to reset a PC back to the place where it comes from. The problem has much similarity with the reconstruction of the topicalization, in connection with which it was also necessary to make a decision about the exact place where it should be considered to have been generated. A difference, however, is that a topicalized constituent never is a subconstituent, since, in that case, subjacency would have been violated. Extraposition only has to pass the border of VP and thus may concern a lower adjoined constituent. This, mainly, causes the difficulties for reconstruction. Another source of problems is the fact that a rather minute analysis of semantic feature combinations is necessary to discard certain hypotheses about the original place of an extrapositioned constituent. Look at the examples of (2):

(2) Daar zag ik de man met de verrekijker.
(There saw I the man with the binoculars)
Daar zag ik de man met de hoed.
(... with the hat)

We need not look for more complicated constructions, to conclude that details of semantic feature specifications as regards lexical items may be decisive for reconstructing a sentence constituent, and rather an NC postmodifier. With a predominant interest in syntactic matters, one may not be extremely appealed to try to solve things like these, and that is the reason certain issues often have to wait. But in a complete interpreter the problem will have to be solved in order to yield satisfactory semantic analyses.

Another subject in the environment of the verb that will have to be treated still is clitic movement. There are certain situations where the basic order of sentence constituents has been disturbed by this movement in such a way, that the assigning of semantic functions is obstructed. The sequence of case functions in

(3) ... toen we 't 'm lieten zien
(... when we it him showed)

is deviating in showing the objective in front of a dative NC, and asks for a transformational reconstruction before the assigning of semantic functions can take place. There seem to be still other movements like quantifier floating (Coppen, forthcoming) that should be analyzed before the interpreter may be considered to be complete. Nevertheless, it is obviously the environment of the V that is especially elaborate. The WH-movement and topicalization are under control, and so are the verb raising and the raising of constituents to subject and object positions. The attributes are connected with the correct NC's, separation of verbal parts is reconstructed adequately and a great deal of semantic dummy constituents do not cause any more trouble. These are the main subjects in syntactic theory and their solution may be considered as a success.

At several places in the foregoing sections it became clear, that optional parts of a verbal construction - operators of place and time and parts with different logical functions - often cause severe problems for the semantic interpretation, since there seems to be no solid theory about the places in the construction where they can be generated. Without any doubt, there are certain places where they cannot appear, for instance at the left side of a dative, but they may precede the objective and, in that way, interfere with case carriers. For a correct interpretation we should know more about this question, and, certainly, we will have to explore the problem before being able to improve the system.

A full development of the semantic interpreter must imply making full use of the features of SELANCA, which means that the theory about the other semantic kernels, N and A, should be extended. As our description shows, not much work has been done with respect to these subjects as yet. The functions needed to describe the N kernel have not been explored. The only function that is present is the attribute. Because of it's being raised to the level of a verbal construction, we met the attribute while working in the environment of the V, and, by lowering it to the N environment, we built something that may be considered as a part of the theory of the N semantic kernel. In very much the same way a first step was made in developing a theory about the A kernel, when an NC that occurred in the V environment, was lowered to the level of the attribute that was subcategorized by the verb and attached to it as an objective function.

As is shown in the appendix, AMAZON(83) is fully equiped to parse coordination constructions. CASUS, however, is not. It will be a major project for the near future to build facilities to interpret coordinated constructions whith gapping, characterized by the fact that certain constituents are missing:

(4) Bart kuste Elly en Henk Mathilde.
(Bart kissed Elly and Henk Mathilde)

It will be important that *Henk* and *Mathilde* are specified as agens and objective respectively of a missing (?) *kuste*. The transformational or rather interpretative theory to be chosen for a solution is only of secondary importance.

It is clear that indicating the lacks and shortcomings of the system is, at the same time, pointing at new research topics. Application oriented research should stick to it's aims and not yield for the temptation to look for new issues because of decreasing courage to finish successfully the old ones. It puts heavier claims to the researcher than does developing theories. Computational linguistics ought to urge a thorough implementation and application of theories, long after the time theoreticians have vanished in far distances, hurried on by great new concepts. It is a science at work. It is not the high flight of thoughts that counts but rather the modest and often unthankful work of building and testing parts of theory with all the difficulties included. Investigating the lacks of what has been achieved is necessary to see how long is still the way ahead. It is our intention to continue the work within the AMAZON-CASUS framework, realizing that the model is incomplete in many respects and that still a lot of work has to be done. We are aware of the fact that, in order to be usable, a system that is able to indicate all linguistic meanings of a sentence should also be capable of adequately selecting one of the meanings indicated in pragmatic situations. How interesting it may be to have all ambiguities specified correctly - and I think it an interesting feature of the developed system that it is indeed capable to do so - it is necessary for any application to go a step further and make a choice after that specification. This necessity, which is recognized by everybody, is often used as a reason to cut short the problem by skipping a try to indicate all possible meanings and by choosing one of them immediately. Obviously, it is often thought to be a less serious shortage that not all interpretations are given than that no clear answer should be obtained. Of course, there is always a possibility to solve the difficulty on the basis of probability, but I think every system should show that it can choose after rather than before summing up the possible choices. The relevance of the work that is reported in this study seems to be, that it shows what are the difficulties of designing an automatic semantic interpreter which has the power to indicate all linguistic meanings of a sentence. These difficulties are of different nature: some have to do with reconstruction of 'deep' structures because of the transformational history of the sentence, others depend upon rather subtle semantic distinctions. In the present study syntax was the central issue. It is our conviction that semantics can only be based upon syntax, and that a thorough syntactic analysis of the sentence should be a fundamental part of every semantic interpretation. That an analyzing system should consist of two components, like ours does, seems to be a self-evident matter and that the first of these may be a contextfree grammar cannot be astonishing. That the second is a computer program, however, perhaps is. It may seem to be possible sometime, to obtain semantic interpretations, like our system yields, from an autonomous grammar, possibly an extended affix grammar. For the time being, the program CASUS shows what will have to be claimed from such an instrument as soon as it will be built. May that be a sufficient account of our project and of the way we tried to reach our goals.

# Notes

1 The way computational linguistics is often looked at (at least in the Netherlands) gives the impression that it might still be relevant to quote Brandt Corstius [1978, 180] who sets out a scale of smaller or greater theoretic involvement and pretention in linguistic research. The work of Chomsky, he says, is to be seen as theory of theory, that of e.g. Evers and Huybregts [1977] as practice of theory, his own study about computational linguistics as theory of practice and computational linguistics itself as practice of practice.

2 See for the proof of this proposition H. Brandt Corstius, [1974], page 96.

3 Cfr. my paper Van Bakel [1983b] with some remarks about the possibility and the applicability of automatic sentence generation and analysis.

4 A classic example is Winograd [1972], who may be quoted in this context: *We assume that a computer cannot deal reasonably with language unless it can understand the subject it is discussing. Therefore, the program is given a detailed model of a particular domain* (T. Winograd [1972, 1]).

5 I realize that my description is somewhat simplified. I refer to Landsbergen [1981] and to the papers of the PHLIQA project mentioned there. See also Scha [1983].

6 The reader is referred to some remarks about the relation of syntax and semantics in Van Bakel [1983b].

7 Schank [1975, 4] is thinking of *meaning representations that could make predictions in order to guide parsing*. This means that semantics is considered to be primary in relation with syntax. In Schank [1972, 560] it is even called *unnecessary to do complete syntactic analysis of a sentence in order to process it conceptually*. These opinions do not seem to be compatible with a linguistic approach.

8 It is not my intention to shift the discussion to the field of A.I. Neither am I intended to fully honour the slighter or grater differences that exist between different authors in that territory. Mainly it can be observed that it's relevance for linguistic phenomena is less than for cognition and psychology. I confine myself to referring globally to: Webber et al. [1978], Burton [1976], Schank [1975], Schank [1972], Wilensky and Arens [1980]. It will become clear what the differences are with my own view.

9 Brandt Corstius [1974, 75] gives the example:

(1) Deze boeren, boeven, boeken ... in respectievclijk Boelgarije, Boeroendi, Boekarest ... zijn respectievelijk woest, jaloers, goedkoop, ...

In order to be grammatical, the '...' must be replaced by three times the same number of constituents. The non-contextfree figure is of the type $a^n b^n c^n$.

10 It has to be added that not offering all possible lexicalizations will possibly prevent AMAZON from assigning one or more syntactic structures to an input sentence, which would come to light if all implications of lexicon and syntax together should be considered. Hence, choosing a lexical interpretation means selecting a subset of the language defined. It is difficult to establish whether an interesting (or rather stupid) part of the language disappears in that way.

11 The second structure interprets the PC *van Marie* as a constituent of UL of VC. The sentence is ambiguous as a parallel of one of the following sentences:

(2) Jan had van Marie gehouden.
Jan had gehouden van Marie.
(John had loved Mary.)

The first sentence shows the PC under MI, the second under UL.

12 It should be pointed out that, in 1975, it was of course not more difficult than whenever else to build some contextfree syntax for Dutch surface structures, but, since we could not dispose of a parser generator, we had to define the grammar in the form of a SNOBOL computer program. Working in that way, we were able to bring in a lot of refining details, whose theoretical status (contextfree or not) was quite obscure. This made it difficult to catch all structures in a contextfree grammar. There are some minor differences left between the earlier and the later form of the grammar.

13 Schank claims: *that there exists a conceptual base that is interlingual, onto which linguistic structures in a given language map during the understanding process and out of which such structures are created during generation*. Schank [1972, 553-554]. A statement of almost the same purport is: *We thus began our search for an interlingua that might be the basis of human thought* [Schank 1975, 8]. The interlingua cannot be the basis, since it will have to be described in turn by some language, which should be independent from natural language.

14 As long as a natural language has not been given the formal state of a programming language, like is the case e.g. in Winograd's [1972] system, the meaning will not be objectively verifiable. The only way to evaluate the results of machine translation from one natural language into another is asking the opinion of bilingual (native) speakers of both languages.

15 My view is largely in accordance with the Whorfian hypothesis about the relations between language and culture. See Whorf [1956].

16 This statement seems to be a total negation of the objectiveness of reality and so it is. Just as in modern physics it is considered to be senseless to relate objects which are receding from each other with more than the speed of light, it is senseless to postulate realities which are not conceived of. Inconceived is a reality that is not represented in any meaning system;

inconceivable is a 'reality' that cannot be represented in a meaning system. That is the reason why realities differ from language to language. Note, that this does not mean that the only way for a reality to be conceived of is being referred to by natural language. It is possible to form a concept of something by perceiving it by means of the sense-organs. In this respect it makes sense to consider natural language as an extension of the human body.

17 In Schank [1975, 97] some remarks are made about the CD (conceptual dependency) representation which was introduced first by Schank [1972]: *The overall criterion is that CD graphs should differ if and only if the meaning being represented differs, excepting differences to logical connectes. It is thus intended that two sentences have the same CD representation if and only if they are paraphrases.* It is implied in the discussion about SELANCA that, according to my opinion, it is only possible to say that two sentences are paraphrases if, in some meaning system, the same representation is built of their meanings.

18 The term knowledge representation, used frequently in A.I. research reports, suggests that knowledge is something rigid and static. I think knowledge itself is to be characterized by a grammar rather than by a list of items, since it seems to be impossible to give a limited definition of any knowledge about any subject. In other words, there is no subject the knowledge about which can be characterized completely in a finite set of sentences. In this way, knowledge shares some important features with reality.

19 Note that the constituents that are not subcategorized by the semantic kernel are interpreted semantically on the same level as where the subcategorized constituents appear, so the set of arguments differs from the elements building the *functional structure* in Jackendoff [1972].

20 I refer to the discussion about interpretative and generative semantics in Jackendoff [1972] and King [1976].

21 By Jackendoff [1972, 1] also meaning of a sentence is viewed as a non-linguistic phenomenon, since supposing a universal semantic representation is *to make an important claim about the innateness of semantic structure, The semantic representation, it is reasonable to hope, is very tightly integrated into the cognitive system of the human mind.* The phrase quoted is a part of a discussion about Katz and Fodor [1963], but seems to reflect also the ideas of the author. With this statement he comes rather near to Schank [1975, 8], who searches for an interlingua *that might be the basis of human thought.* As may be concluded from the present section, I disagree. I think it correcter to say, that the only means to represent the contents of human mind is natural language. Or put otherwise: natural language is the way human mind reveals itself. Cfr. note 16.

22 See Salemans and Bouhof [1981].

23 This restriction seems to be rather accidental, as is shown by an observation as:

(3) Wie zich daar ophoudt, heb ik het gissen naar.
(Benno Barnard, *Klein Rozendaal*, Arbeiderspers 1984.)

Less aberrant forms for this sentence are:

(4) Ik heb er het gissen naar, wie zich daar ophoudt.
Ik heb het gissen ernaar, wie zich daar ophoudt.
Ik heb het gissen, wie zich daar ophoudt.

In NRC's Cultureel Supplement of 17 February 1984, Wiel Kusters writes: *Hoe kan iemand zo'n verwrongen zin opschrijven?*, to which he adds a (superfluous) psychological explanation. It is obvious that the only cause of the aberrance is the application of an unapplicable topicalization.

24 In this connection the question is raised about the possibility of semantically empty syntactic rules. The subject will be touched upon in section 3.2.1.10.

25 In the example sentences no effort is made to distinguish systematically the different forms the attributes can take. The following are to be mentioned: adjective, past participle, preposition phrase, conjunctional phrase with *als* (as), noun phrase, and other more complex constituents too, e.g.:

(5) *De handen in de schoot* zat zij voor zich uit te staren.
(The hands in the lap sat she for herself to stare)
With folded arms she sat staring ahead.

I do not intend to deal with all details. The theory is powerful enough to handle all forms except the last.

26 Note, that the small clause has still another reading, namely:

(6) [S als financieel-economisch deskundige [NP werkzaam bij de directie kunsten van WVC]] ...

Here NP means: postmodifier.

27 In Chomsky [1981, 109-110] no attention is paid to the question of the syntactic state of *as*. I think the argumentation about the small clause connected with *regard*, given as [S NP *as* ...], is not convincing in as far the position of *as* is concerned. However, Chomsky's argumentation needs almost no change, when *as* is considered as a conjunction that governs the small clause: *as* [S NP ...].

28 This observation was made by Van Wijk-Van Schothorst, *De Nederlandsche Taal*, Zwolle 1931, pag. 51.

29 The test of the fourth sequence under the hypothesis of the first case frame (+WH and −WH) of the verb *vond*, however, does not fail, although the word *vaak* (often) does not meet the claims of the case ATT(ribute). The 'severe' rule has to accept an intervening operator.

30 Geer Hoppenbrouwers (Provisional draft of a fragment of *Algemeen Nederlandse Spraakkunst*: Werkwoorden met een verbaal complement) characterizes the differences by distinguishing verbs with obliged clustering, verbs with optional clustering and verbs without clustering:

(7) Hij beweerde dat hij de kraanvogels *zou fotograferen*
a. Hij zei dat hij *probeerde* de vogels *te filmen*
b. Hij zei dat hij de vogels *probeerde te filmen*
Hij zei dat hij zich *verheugde* de vogels *te zien*.

See also Rijpma-Schuringa-Van Bakel [1978, 203-211] about unseparable verbal clusters.

31 In a sentence like (8)

(8) Jan beval Anna naar de dominee te luisteren.
(John ordered Ann to listen to the vicar.)

for which no verb raising should be hypothesized, the border between the matrix and the S-complement is also transparant.

32 The diagram (9) shows the category name PV in stead of the expected '12'; see tree (8). In order to produce uniform output, CASUS changes the symbols for semi-auxiliaries.

33 I consider the constituent *weer* (again) in (13)b as raised, although it is not an NC.

34 One more difficulty is added, when an operator like *luidkeels* has been topicalized. Look at sentence (9):

(9) Luidkeels had Peter Mariet het volkslied horen zingen.

As is argued in section 3.2.1.8, the topicalized constituent will have to be tested on every place where it possibly has been generated. Since it may be a constituent of both the matrix and the S complement, we will have to replace it towards positions of both constructions. Since these have been mixed by raising, we will have to test it on all places of both sets of constituents (according to (15)) appearing at the one surface-level construction. In section 3.2.1.8, however, arguments have been given for testing an operator only once, namely on the extreme right position. The considerations, explained in the present context, are to be connected with those of section 3.2.1.8.

35 Peter-Arno Coppen (forthcoming 2) gives a formal characterization of ambiguity, which shows some interesting differences with mine.

36 Barbara Partee [1973] assumes, that Montague grammar should admit some kind of move-α, that should stay outside the compositionallity principle in that it is not correlated with a semantic rule.

# References


**Barwise and Perry (1983)**
Jon Barwise and John Perry, *Situations and Attitudes*, MIT Press, Cambridge and London, 1983.

**Brandt Corstius (1974)**
H. Brandt Corstius, *Algebraische Taalkunde*, Utrecht 1974.

**Brandt Corstius (1978)**
H. Brandt Corstius, *Computer-Taalkunde*, Muiderberg 1978.

**Burton (1976)**
R. Burton, *Semantic Grammar: An Engineering Technique for Constructing Natural Language Understanding Systems*, Technical Report 3453, Cambridge MA, Bolt Beranek and Newman Inc. 1976.

**Burton and Brown (1977)**
Richard R. Burton, John Seely Brown, *Semantic Grammar: A Technique for Construction Natural Language Interfaces to Structural Systems*, BBN Report No. 3587, Bolt Beranek and Newman Inc. May 1977.

**Chomsky (1957)**
Noam Chomsky, *Syntactic Structures*, Mouton Den Haag, 1957.

**Chomsky (1965)**
Noam Chomsky, *Aspects of the Theory of Syntax*, MIT Press, Cambridge 1965.

**Chomsky (1979)**
Noam Chomsky, On markedness and core grammar. In: A. Belletti, L. Brandi and L.Rizzi, eds., *Theory of Markedness in Generative Grammar*, Proceedings of the 1979 GLOW conference, Pisa 1981.

**Chomsky (1981)**
Noam Chomsky, *Lectures on Government and Binding*, Foris Dordrecht 1981.

**Coppen (forthcoming)**
P.A. Coppen, *De aard van het quantitatieve* **er**; unpublished paper, KUN Nijmegen, Dep. of Computational Linguistics.

**Coppen (forthcomming; 2)**
Peter-Arno Coppen, *Ambiguïteit en Computerlinguïstiek*, unpublished paper, KUN Nijmegen, Dep. of Computational Linguistics, presented at the Nederlands Filologencongres, Nijmegen 1984.

**Evers and Huybregts (1977)**
A. Evers and M.A.C. Huybregts, *Transformationele Kerngrammatika's van het Nederlands en het Duits*, Utrecht 1977.

**Fillmore (1968)**
Ch. Fillmore, The Case for Case; in: Bach and Harms, (eds.), *Universals in Linguistic Theory*, 1968, 1-88.

**Friedman (1971)**
Joyce Friedman a.o., *A Computer Model of Transformational Grammar*, Elsevier New York, 1971.

**Gazdar (1979)**
Gerald Gazdar, *Constituent Structures*, Paper January 1979; 49 pages.

**Huiskens and Wever (1983)**
Lucie Huiskens and Patrick Wever, Reconstructie van scheidbare werkwoorden; in: *Verslagen Computerlinguïstiek*, No. 3 (1983), 115-123.

**Jackendoff (1972)**
Ray S. Jackendoff, *Semantic Interpretation in Generative Grammar*, MIT Press, Cambridge, London, 1972.

**Jackendoff (1976)**
R. Jackendoff, Toward an explanatory semantic representation; in: *Linguistic Inquiry*, 7, 1, 89-150, 1976.

**Kempen and Hoenkamp (1982)**
G. Kempen and E. Hoenkamp, An incremental procedural Grammar for sentence formulation; unpublished report KU Nijmegen 1982, *Cognitive Science*, forthcoming.

**King (1976)**
Margaret King, Generative Semantics; in: Eugene Charniak and Yorick Wilks, eds. *Computational Semantics, An Introduction to Artificial Intelligence and Natural Language Comprehension*, North-Holland Publishing Company, Amsterdam 1976, 73-88.

**Katz and Fodor [1963]**
Jerold J. Katz and Jerry Fodor, The Structure of a Semantic Theory, *Language* 39, 170-210.

**Klieverik (1983)**
Harry Klieverik, TPASSIEF voor KASUS(82); in: *Verslagen Computerlinguïstiek*, No. 3 (1983), 41-64.

**Koster (1978)**
J. Koster, *Locality Principles in Syntax*, Thesis, University of Amsterdam, 1978.

KOSTER (1983)
Jan Koster, De ontsemiotisering van het wereldbeeld, *Gramma, Nijmeegs Tijdschrift voor Taalkunde*, 7(1983), 2/3 309-329.

KRAAK AND KLOOSTER (1968)
A.C. Kraak and W. Klooster, *Syntaxis*, Culemborg Keulen 1968.

KRIPKE (1972)
S. Kripke, Naming and Necessity; in: D. Davidson and G. Harman, eds., *Semantics of Natural Language* Reidel, Dordrecht, 1972.

LANDSBERGEN (1981)
Jan Landsbergen, Adaptation of Montague Grammar to the Requirements of Parsing; in: J.A.G. Groenendijk, T.M.V. Janssen and M.B.J. Stokhof (eds.), *Formal Methods in the Study of Language*, Amsterdam, Mathematisch Centrum 1981, p. 399-419.

MARCUS (1980)
Mitchell P. Marcus, *A Theory of Syntactic Recognition for Natural Language*, MIT Press, Cambridge MA and London, 1980.

MARCUS (1981)
Mitchell Marcus, A computational account of some constraints on language; in: Joshi, Webber and Sag, eds., *Elements of Discourse Understanding*, 1981, p. 177 - 200.

MONTAGUE (1973)
R. Montague, The proper treatment of quantification in ordinary English. In: J. Hintikka e.a. (eds.), *Approaches to Natural Language*, Dordrecht 1973.

PARTEE (1973)
Barbara Partee, Some Transformational Extensions of Montague Grammar, *Journal of Philosophical Logic*, 2(1973), 509-534.

REICHLING (1935)
Dr. Anton Reichling, *Het Woord, een studie omtrent de grondslag van taal en taalgebruik*, Nijmegen 1935.

REINTJES (1983)
Pieter Reintjes, Reconstructie van Topicalisatie; in: *Verslagen Computerlinguïstiek*, No. 3 (1983), 74-96.

RIJPMA-SCHURINGA-VAN BAKEL (1978)
E. Rijpma, F.G. Schuringa, Jan van Bakel, *Nederlandse Spraakkunst*, Groningen 1978.

SALEMANS AND BOUHOF (1981)
Ben Salemans and Marcel Bouhof, References: Een theorie over anaforische relaties binnen AMAZON; in: *Verslagen Computerlinguïstiek*, 2(1981), 58-90.

SCHA (1983)
Remko J.H. Scha, *Logical Foundations for Question Answering*, diss. Groningen, Philips, Eindhoven 1983.

SCHANK (1972)
R. Schank, Conceptual Dependency: A Theory of Natural Language Understanding, *Cognitive Psychology*, 1972, 3, 552-631.

SCHANK (1975)
R.C. Schank, *Conceptual Information Processing*, American Elsevier Publishing Company, Inc., New York 1975.

SCHOLTEN, EVERS AND KLEIN (1980)
T. Scholten, Arn. Evers and M. Klein, *Inleiding in de Transformationeel-generatieve taaltheorie*, Groningen 1981.

SIMMONS (1973)
R.F. Simmons, Semantic Networks: Their Computation and Use for Understanding English Sentences; in: Schank and Colby, eds., *Computer Models of Thought and Language*, 1973.

VAN BAKEL (1975)
Jan van Bakel, *Automatische Zinsontleding met de Computer*, KU Nijmegen, 1975.

VAN BAKEL AND HOOGEBOOM (1981)
Jan van Bakel and Sietse Hoogeboom, Eksperiment met een Kasusgrammatika; in: *Verslagen Computerlinguïstiek* No. 2 (1981), 1 - 57.

VAN BAKEL (1981)
Jan van Bakel, Een nieuwe versie van AMAZON; in; *Verslagen Computerlinguïstiek*, No.2 (1981), 91-105.

VAN BAKEL (1982)
Jan van Bakel, Automatic Analysis of WH-Movement in Dutch, *ITL Review of Applied Linguistics*, 1982, 45-81.

VAN BAKEL (1983A)
Jan van Bakel, Depassivisering e.a. in CASUS(82); in: *Verslagen Computerlinguïstiek*, No. 3 (1983), 65-73.

VAN BAKEL (1983B)
Jan van Bakel, Methodologie van de Computerlinguïstiek, *Gramma, Nijmeegs Tijdschrift voor Taalkunde*, 7(1983), 2/3 175-188.

VAN OPSTAL (1983)
Toon van Opstal, *Verbale Verstrengeling*, undergraduate study report Computational Lnguistics 1983, KU Nijmegen.

**Webber et. al (1978)**
B.L. Webber, R. Bobrow, W.A. Woods, Report No. 3878: *Research in Natural Language Understanding*; Quarterly Progress Report No. 3, 1 March 1978 to 31 May 1978; Bolt Beranek and Newman Inc., Cambridge MA 02138.

**Wever (1984)**
Patrick Wever, *Interpretatie van S-complementen onder CASUS*, undergraduate study report Computational Linguistics 1984, KU Nijmegen, forthcoming.

**Whorf (1956)**
B.L. Whorf, *Language, Thought and Reality: Selected Writings of Benjamin Lee Whorf*, J.B. Carroll (ed.), MIT Press, Cambridge.

**Williams (1975)**
E. Williams, Small Clauses in English; in: J. Kimball, ed. *Syntax and Semantics*, vol. 4, Academic Press, 1975.

**Wilensky and Arens (1980)**
Robert Wilensky and Yigel Arens, PHRAN, A Knowledge-Based Natural Language Understander; in: *The 18th Annual Meeting of the Association for Computational Linguistics and Parasession on Topics in Interactive Discourse*, Proceedings of the Conference, June 19-22, 1980, University of Pennsylvania, Philadelphia, 1980, 117-121.

**Wilks (1977)**
Yorick Wilks, Natural Language Understanding systems within the A.I. Paradigm: A Survey and Some Comparisons; in: Antonio Zampolli, ed., *Linguistic Structures Processing*, North-Holland Publishing Company, Amsterdam 1977, 341-398.

**Winograd (1972)**
Terry Winograd, Understanding Natural Language, *Cognitive Psychology*, 1972, 1-191.

# Appendix

## 1 AMAZON

### A. Syntactic Rules

```
(1) S0                    : SE,".".

(2) AJ                    : evbw<gradv>0,AK,evcj<"1">0.
(3) evbw<gradv>0          : BW<gradv>;empty0.
(4) CJ<"1">               : NV,AJ.

(5) evcj<a>0              : CJ<a>;empty0.
(6) NV                    : nvgw0.

(7) AK                    : adj0,evcj<"2">0.
(8) CJ<"2">               : NV,AK.

(9) AV                    : advprt0.
(10) BW<adv>              : bw0,evcj<"3">0;AK.
(11) CJ<"3">              : NV,BW<adv>.
(12) BW<relatief>         : reladv0,evcj<"4">0.
(13) CJ<"4">              : NV,BW<relatief>.
(14) BW<gradv>            : gradv0;gradv0,BW<gradv>.

(15) eerste0              : CC<"1">;CC<"2">;BW<adv>;BW<relatief>;
        PC<"0">;PC<relatief>;NC<nietrelatief,"0">;NC<relatief,"0">;
        NC<w1>;AJ;W1<relatiefmidden,"0">;W2<"0">;W3<"0">;W4<"0">;
        W5<"0">.

(16) CL<"1">              : v<"0">0;v<"2">0,c<"2">0;
        c<"2">0,v<"2">0;VD,v12,v24;VD,v12,v23,v34;v<"3">0,c<"3">0;
        c<"3">0,v<"3">0;VD,v13,v34;VD,v13,v33,v34;
        VD,v13,v32,v23,v34;v<"4">0,c<"4">0;c<"4">0,v<"4">0.
(17) CL<"2">              : c<"2">0.
(18) c<"2">0              : VI<ti>;v23,VI;v23,v33,VI;
        v23,v33,v33,VI;v23,v34,v33,VI;v24,v33,VI;v24,v33,v33,VI;
        v24,VD;VD,v24;v23,v34,VD;v23,VD,v34;VD,v23,v34.
(19) CL<"3">              : c<"3">0.
(20) c<"3">0              : VI;v33,VI;v33,v33,VI;v34,v33,VI;
```

v33,v34,v33,VI;v32,v23,VI;v32,v23,v33,VI;v32,v23,v34,v33,VI; v32,v24,v33,VI;v32,VI<ti>;v33,v32,VI<ti>;v34,v33,v32,VI<ti>; v34,VD;VD,v34;v33,v34,VD;v33,VD,v34;VD,v33,v34; v32,v23,v34,VD;v32,v23,VD,v34;v32,VD,v23,v34;VD,v32,v23,v34.

(21) CL<"4"> : c<"4">0.

(22) c<"4">0 : VD;v33,VI;v33,v33,v32,VI<ti>; v33,v32,VI<ti>;v33,v33,VI;v32,VI<ti>.

(23) CL<"4",wwcon> : VD.

(24) CL<"5"> : TD;v54,VD;VD,v54;v53,v34,VD; v53,VD,v34;VD,v53,v34;v53,VI;v53,v33,VI;v52,VI;v52,v23,VI; v52,v23,v33,VI;v52,v24,v33,VI;v52,v23,v34,v33,VI;v52,v24,VD; v52,VD,v24;VD,v52,v24.

(25) VI<ti> : vsubti0,evcj<"5">0.

(26) VI : vsubi0,evcj<"6">0.

(27) CJ<"5"> : NV,VI<ti>.

(28) CJ<"6"> : NV,VI.

(29) LW<relatief> : quis0.

(30) evlw<nietrelatief>0 : LW<nietrelatief>;empty0.

(31) LW<nietrelatief> : lw0;attripr0.

(32) MI<relatief,0tm2> : mi<releerste,0tm2>0,mid<0tm2>0; mi<releerste,0tm2>0.

(33) mid<0tm2>0 : middendelen<0tm2>0; middendelen<0tm2>0,AV;AV.

(34) midden<0tm2>0 : MI<0tm2>;empty0.

(35) MI<0tm2> : mid<0tm2>0.

(36) mi<releerste,"0">0 : NC<relatief,"1">;BW<relatief>; PC<relatief>.

(37) mi<releerste,"1">0 : NC<relatief,"2">;PC<relatief>; BW<relatief>.

(38) mi<releerste,"2">0 : BW<relatief>.

(39) middendelen<0tm2>0 : middendeel<0tm2>0,middendelen<0tm2>0; middendeel<0tm2>0.

(40) middendeel<"0">0 : AJ;CC<"2">;BW<adv>;PC<"1">; NC<nietrelatief,"1">.

(41) middendeel<"1">0 : BW<adv>.

(42) middendeel<"2">0 : empty0.

(43) NC<w1> : W1<relatiefmidden,"0">.

(44) NC<relatief,0tm2> : LW<relatief>,evna<0tm2>0,NK<noun>, evnp0,evcj<"7">0;evlw<nietrelatief>0,evna<0tm2>0,NK<noun>, NP<relatief>,evcj<"7">0;evlw<nietrelatief>0,NK<relatief>, evnp0,evcj<"7">0.

(45) CJ<"7"> : NV,NC<relatief,"0">.

(46) NC<nietrelatief,0tm2> : LW<nietrelatief>,NK<pronomen>,

```
        evnp<relatievebijzin>0,evcj<"8">0;evlw<nietrelatief>0,
        evna<0tm2>0,NK<noun>,evnp0,evcj<"8">0.
(47) CJ<"8">                 : NV,NC<nietrelatief,"0">.
(48) CJ<"9">                 : NV,NC<nietrelatief,"1">.
(49) CJ<"10">                : NV,NC<nietrelatief,"2">.

(50) evna<0tm2>0             : NA<0tm2>;empty0.
(51) NA<0tm2>                : nad<0tm2>0.
(52) nad<0tm2>0              : ncadeel<0tm2>0,nad<0tm2>0;
        ncadeel<0tm2>0.
(53) ncadeel<0tm2>0          : W2<0tm2,"nca">;W4<0tm2,"nca">;
        W5<0tm2,"nca">;TW<"0">;AJ.

(54) NK<noun>                : n0;pron0.
(55) NK<pronomen>            : attripr0;adj0.
(56) NK<relatief>            : quod0.

(57) evnp0                   : NP;empty0.
(58) NP                      : PC<"0">;W1<relatiefmidden,"0">;
        PC<"0">,W1<relatiefmidden,"0">;W2<np>;W4<np>;W5<np>.
(59) NP<relatief>            : PC<relatief>,evnp0.
(60) evnp<relatievebijzin>0  : NP<relatievebijzin>;empty0.
(61) NP<relatievebijzin>     : W1<relatiefmidden,"0">.

(62) PC<0tm2>                : VZ,NC<nietrelatief,0tm2>,evcj<"15">0;
        VZ,NC<w1>,evcj<"15">0;VZ,W2<"0">,evcj<"15">0.
(63) PC<relatief>            : VZ,NC<relatief,"1">,evcj<"16">0.
(64) VZ                      : vrz0.
(65) CJ<"15">                : NV,PC<"1">.
(66) CJ<"16">                : NV,PC<relatief>.

(67) v<"0">0                 : PV,evcj<"18">0.
(68) v<"2">0                 : v12,evcj<"19">0.
(69) v<"3">0                 : v13,evcj<"20">0.
(70) v<"4">0                 : v14,evcj<"21">0.
(71) CJ<"18">                : NV,v<"0">0.
(72) CJ<"19">                : NV,v<"2">0.
(73) CJ<"20">                : NV,v<"3">0.
(74) CJ<"21">                : NV,v<"4">0.

(75) SE                      : eveerste0,VC<x>,evcj<"17">0.
(76) eveerste0               : eerste0;empty0.
(77) CJ<"17">                : NV,SE.

(78) TD                      : tdw0,evcj<"11">0.
(79) v52                     : hvtitd0,evcj<"12">0.
(80) v53                     : hvitd0,evcj<"13">0.
```

```
(81) v54                    : hvttd0,evcj<"14">0.
(82) CJ<"11">               : NV,TD.
(83) CJ<"12">               : NV,v52.
(84) CJ<"13">               : NV,v53.
(85) CJ<"14">               : NV,v54.

(86) TW<"0">                : TW<"1">,TW<"1">;TW<"1">.
(87) TW<"1">                : rtelw0;htelw0.

(88) evul0                  : UL;empty0.
(89) UL                     : CC<"1">;CC<"2">;
        W1<relatiefmidden,"0">;W2<ul>;W4<ul>;W5<ul>;PC<"0">;
        PC<"0">,CC<"1">;PC<"0">,W1<relatiefmidden,"0">;
        PC<"0">,W2<"0">;PC<"0">,W4<"0">;PC<"0">,W5<"0">;
        W1<relatiefmidden,"0">,CC<"1">;
        W1<relatiefmidden,"0">,CC<"2">.

(90) VC<"0">                : v<"0">0,midden<"0">0,evul0.
(91) VC<"2">                : v<"2">0,midden<"0">0,CL<"2">,evul0.
(92) VC<"3">                : v<"3">0,midden<"0">0,CL<"3">,evul0.
(93) VC<"4">                : v<"4">0,midden<"0">0,CL<"4">,evul0.

(94) VD                     : vdw0,evcj<"22">0.
(95) CJ<"22">               : NV,VD.

(96) CC<"1">
        : VW<"1">,W1<nietrelatiefmidden,"0">,evcj<"23">0.
(97) CC<"2">                : VW<"2">,W1<nietrelatiefmidden,"0">.
(98) VW<"1">                : grvgw0.
(99) VW<"2">                : vgw0.
(100) CJ<"23">              : NV,CC<"1">.
(101) CJ<"24">              : NV,CC<"2">.

(102) W1<nietrelatiefmidden,0tm2>
        :midden<0tm2>0,CL<"1">,evul0,evcj<"25">0.
(103) W1<relatiefmidden,0tm2>
        : MI<relatief,0tm2>,CL<"1">,evul0,evcj<"26">0.
(104) CJ<"25">              : NV,W1<nietrelatiefmidden,"0">.
(105) CJ<"26">              : NV,W1<relatiefmidden,"0">.
(106) W2<0tm2>
        : midden<0tm2>0,CL<"2">,evul0,evcj<"27">0.
(107) CJ<"27">              : NV,W2<"0">.
(108) W3<0tm2>
        : midden<0tm2>0,CL<"3">,evul0,evcj<"28">0.
(109) CJ<"28">              : NV,W3<"0">.
(110) W4<0tm2>
        : midden<0tm2>0,CL<"4",wwcon>,evul0,evcj<"29">0.
```

```
(111) CJ<"29">              : NV,W4<"0">.
(112) W5<0tm2>
        : midden<0tm2>0,CL<"5">,evul0,evcj<"30">0.
(113) CJ<"30">              : NV,W5<"0">.
(114) W2<0tm2,"nca">        : midden<0tm2>0,CL<"2">,evcj<"31">0.
(115) CJ<"31">              : NV,W2<"0","nca">.
(116) W4<0tm2,"nca">        : midden<0tm2>0,CL<"4">,evcj<"32">0.
(117) CJ<"32">              : NV,W4<"0","nca">.
(118) W5<0tm2,"nca">        : midden<0tm2>0,CL<"5">,evcj<"33">0.
(119) CJ<"33">              : NV,W5<"0","nca">.
(120) W2<np>                : MI<"0">,CL<"2">,evul0,evcj<"31">0;
        CL<"2">,UL,evcj<"31">0.
(121) W4<np>                : MI<"0">,CL<"4",wwcon>,evul0,
        evcj<"32">0;CL<"4",wwcon>,UL,evcj<"32">0.
(122) W5<np>                : MI<"0">,CL<"5">,evul0,evcj<"33">0;
        CL<"5">,UL,evcj<"33">0.
```

B. Lexical Rules

```
(123) vsubti0               : "VSUBTI0","(",woord0,")".
(124) vsubi0                : "VSUBI0","(",woord0,")".
(125) vdw0                  : "VDW0","(",woord0,")".
(126) tdw0                  : "TDW0","(",woord0,")".
(127) hvtitd0               : "HVTITD0","(",woord0,")".
(128) hvitd0                : "HVITD0","(",woord0,")".
(129) hvttd0                : "HVTTD0","(",woord0,")".
(130) v12                   : "HVTIP0","(",woord0,")".
(131) v13                   : "HVIP0","(",woord0,")".
(132) v14                   : "HVTP0","(",woord0,")".
(133) PV                    : "VSUBP0","(",woord0,")".
(134) v22                   : "HVTITI0","(",woord0,")".
(135) v23                   : "HVITI0","(",woord0,")".
(136) v24                   : "HVTTI0","(",woord0,")".
(137) v32                   : "HVTII0","(",woord0,")".
(138) v33                   : "HVII0","(",woord0,")".
(139) v34                   : "HVTI0","(",woord0,")".
(140) nvgw0                 : "NVGW0","(",woord0,")".
(141) adj0                  : "ADJ0","(",woord0,")".
(142) advprt0               : "ADVPRT0","(",woord0,")".
(143) bw0                   : "BW0","(",woord0,")".
(144) reladv0               : "RELADV0","(",woord0,")".
(145) gradv0                : "GRADV0","(",woord0,")".
(146) quis0                 : "QUIS0","(",woord0,")".
(147) attripr0              : "ATTRIPR0","(",woord0,")".
(148) lw0                   : "LW0","(",woord0,")".
(149) n0                    : "N0","(",woord0,")".
(150) pron0                 : "PRON0","(",woord0,")".
```

(151) quod0 : "QUOD0","(",woord0,")".
(152) vrz0 : "VRZ0","(",woord0,")".
(153) rtelw0 : "RTELW0","(",woord0,")".
(154) htelw0 : "HTELW0","(",woord0,")".
(155) grvgw0 : "GRVGW0","(",woord0,")".
(156) vgw0 : "VGW0","(",woord0,")".

C. Details

(157) woord0 : letter0,woord0;letter0.
(158) letter0 : "A";"B";"C";"D";"E";"F";"G";"H";"I";
"J";"K";"L";"M";"N";"O";"P";"Q";"R";"S";"T";"U";"V";"W";"X";
"Y";"Z";"1";"2";"3";"4";"5";"6";"7";"8";"9";"0";" ".
(159) empty0 : "".

D. Meta Rules

| | | |
|---|---|---|
| (I) | gradv | :: "gradv". |
| (II) | adv | :: "adv". |
| (III) | relatief | :: "relatief". |
| (IV) | releerste | :: "releerste". |
| (V) | nietrelatief | :: "nietrelatief". |
| (VI) | relatiefmidden | :: "relatiefmidden". |
| (VII) | nietrelatiefmidden | "nietrelatiefmidden". |
| (VIII) | relatievebijzin | :: "relatievebijzin". |
| (IX) | wwcon | :: "wwcon". |
| (X) | noun | :: "noun". |
| (XI) | pronomen | :: "pronomen". |
| (XII) | x | :: "0";"2";"3";"4". |
| (XIII) | 0tm2 | :: "0";"1";"2". |
| (XIV) | a | :: "1";"2";"3";"4";"5";"6";"7";"8";"9"; "10";"11";"12";"13";"14";"15";"16";"17";"18";"19";"20";"21"; "22";"23";"24";"25";"26";"27";"28";"29";"30";"31";"32";"33". |
| (XV) | ti | :: "ti". |
| (XVI) | nca | :: "nca". |
| (XVII) | np | :: "np". |
| (XVIII) | ul | :: "np". |
| (XIX) | w1 | :: "w1". |

# 2 CASUS

In this section I describe a number of subroutines of the semantic interpreter CASUS. I will only deal with those functions that are relevant for the linguistic aspects of the program; merely administrative routines will not be commented. The order in which the functions are given is alphabetic. By indicating which functions call which other functions and by which function(s) a certain function is called, the reader is helped to get a good insight in the way the interpreter is organized both globally and in detail.

Functions whose Arguments and/or Returned value(s) are zero, operate on a globally available data object, mostly a part of the sentence's tree structure. Functions that receive pointers as arguments operate in the same way.

No. 1
Function Name: Acceptable cand for case.
Arguments: A pointer to a certain constituent that is a candidate for a case function; the name of the case function concerned; the caseframe concerned of the verb concerned.
Returned value(s): True or False.
Called by: Applicable structure.
Calling: All case claims met ; Match number and person.

No. 2
Function Name: Adapt semi aux construction.
Arguments: A pointer to one of the main verbs of the sentence.
Returned value(s): None.
Called by: Administrate satellites.
Note: The subroutine reconstructs the sentence structure. It adds branches (UL (CC (W2 )) to undo verb raising.

No. 3
Function Name: Administrate satellites.
Arguments: None.
Returned value(s): None.
Called by: Translater.
Calling: Adapt semi aux construction; Set verb features; WH compontop; Find satellites; Allign AV; Delete dummies.

No. 4
Function Name: All case claims met.
Arguments: Pointers to the caseframe concerned of the main verb concerned, to the constituent concerned as a case candidate, a value for the active or passive voice of the S considered, the name of the case function concerned.
Returned value(s): True or False.
Called by: Acceptable cand for case.

Calling: Test claims.

Note: The subroutine tests whether all claims put by the verb as regards the features of a candidate for a certain case are met.

No. 5

Function Name: Allign AV.

Arguments: An array with pointers to the case candidates for the verb concerned and a pointer to the verb concerned.

Returned value(s): None; the sentence structure is changed globally.

Called by: Administrate satellites.

Note: The subroutine brings a separated part of a separable verb back to the verb it belongs to.

No. 6

Function Name: Allign WH component.

Arguments: An index to refer to one of the main verbs of te sentence.

Returned value(s): None.

Called by: Interpret sentence.

Note: If there has been found a WH-constituent that may have a case function in connection with the main verb considered, the subroutine adds it to the set of case candidates if that possibility is to be tested.

No. 7

Function Name: Allocate candidate.

Arguments: A pointer to a case candidate and a value for the case function considered.

Returned value(s): None.

Called by: Applicable structure.

Note: The subroutine administrates that this constituent is to be considered as the elected candidate for the case function concerned.

No. 8

Function Name: Analyse.

Arguments: A string in the form of a labeled bracketing.

Returned value(s) : None.

Called by: Read Sent.

Calling : Analyse (recursively).

Note: The subroutine builds a tree structure on the basis of the input string.

No. 9

Function Name: Applicable structure.

Arguments: A pointer to the array with case candidates, a pointer to main verb considered, a pointer to the caseframe of that verb considered.

Returned value(s): True or False.

Called by: Interpret sentence.

Calling: Acceptable cand for case, Allocate candidate.

Note: The subroutine tests whether a certain caseframe of the main verb considered is applicable to the set of case candidates considered.

No. 10
Function Name: Attrib sent.
Arguments: A pointer to the first element of the array containing the case candidates for the main verb considered.
Returned value(s): True or False.
Called by: Retrieve semantic info and Test sequences.
Note: The subroutine tests whether the S considered is a relative clause.

No. 11
Function Name: Bridge verb.
Arguments: A pointer to one of the main verbs of the sentence.
Returned value(s): True or False.
Called by: Administrate satellites, WH compontop.
Note: The subroutine tests whether the verb pointed at is a socalled bridge verb that admits WH-movement.

No. 12
Function Name: Change sequence casus.
Arguments: An array with pointers to the case candidates, a number to indicate a type of permutation and a string with information about some main properties of the case candidates.
Returned value(s): None.
Called by: Interpret sentence.
Note: The subroutine performs a permutation of the set of case candidates.

No. 13
Function Name: Consult lexicon.
Arguments: A pointer to a node of the tree structure.
Returned value(s): None.
Called by: Translater, Allign AV, Rearrange passive construction.
Calling: Retrieve L I
Note: The subroutine links terminal symbols of the tree structure with elements of the lexicon.

No. 14
Function Name: Delete dummies.
Arguments: An index to refer to a certain main verb and an array with pointers to the case candidates.
Returned value(s): None.
Called by: Administrate satellites.
Calling: Dummy pron
Note: The subroutine deletes dummy pronouns i e.redundant pronouns which are superfluous as case candidates.

No. 15
Function Name: Depassivize.
Arguments: A pointer to the main verb considered, a pointer to the ASPECT of that verb

and a pointer to it's grandfather.
Returned value(s): None.
Called by: Interpret sentence.
Calling: Possibly passive, Test claims, Rearrange passive construction
Note: The subroutine performs depassivization.

No. 16
Function Name: Detopicalize resetverb.
Arguments: A pointer to the top of the tree structure.
Returned value(s): None.
Called by: Translater.
Note: The subroutine performs detopicalization of the sentence and resetting of the finite verb.

No. 17
Function Name: Find kernel.
Arguments: A pointer to a node of the tree structure.
Returned value(s): A pointer to the semantic kernel of the node node pointed at
Called by: Pop lexical information.
Calling: Find kernel (recursively)

No. 18
Function Name: Find nodes.
Arguments: A pointer to a node of the tree structure, a pattern, an index for a depth (optional) and an index for a number (optional).
Returned value(s): An array with pointers to a NUMBER (the last argument) of nodes of the tree, indicated with the first argument of the function.
Called by: Different functions.
Calling: Find nodes (recursively).
Note: The function operates on a certain subtree, whose top is the first argument, looks for subtrees (nodes) with the feature of pattern (second argument) going to a maximal depth (third argument) under the starting point, and collects pointers to the subtrees found, to a maximal number as indicated by the last argument.

No. 19
Function Name: Find satellites.
Arguments: A pointer to a main verb.
Returned value(s): An array with pointers to the case candidates of that main verb.
Called by: Administrate satellites.

No. 20
Function name: Insert PRO.
Arguments: An index, referring to a certain main verb.
Returned value(s): None.
Called by: Interpret sentence.
Note: The function adds a PRO constituent to the case candidates in certain constructions.

No. 21
Function name: Interpret PRO.
Arguments: An index to refer to a certain main verb.
Returned value(s): None.
Note: The function specifies the constituent in the environment with which this PRO has to be associated.

No. 22
Function Name: Interpret sentence.
Arguments: None.
Returned value(s): None.
Called by: Translater.
Calling: Expand case frames, Reset original sequence, Allign WH component, Connect trans nodes, Depassivize, Set index sequences, Change sequence casus, Applicable structure, Connect, Write result.

No. 23
Function Name: Load lexicon.
Arguments: None.
Returned value(s): None.
Called by: Translater.
Calling: Store L I.

No. 24
Function Name: Match number and person.
Arguments: A pointer to a main verb, a pointer to a case candidate, information concerning active or passive voice and information about the status of the main verb (finite or infinite).
Returned value(s): None.
Called by: Acceptable cand for case C.
Calling: Number and person N, Number and person V.
The subroutine controls agreement.

No. 25
Function Name: Semantic Kernel.
Arguments: A pointer to the semantic kernel of a constituent (found by the subroutine Find kernel) and a pointer to that constituent itself.
Returned value(s): None.
Called by: Pop lex information.
Note: The subroutine copies the lexical information of the kernel of a constituent on it's top.

No. 26
Function Name: Number and person N.
Arguments: A pointer to a case candidate and information about passive or active voice.
Returned value(s): Information in string form about number and person of the case candidate.

Called by: Match number and person.

No. 27
Function Name: Number and person V.
Arguments: A pointer to a main verb and information about it's form (finite or infinite).
Returned value(s): Information in string form about the verb's number and person.
Called by: Match number and person.

No. 28
Function Name: Pop lexical information.
Arguments: A pointer to a node of the tree structure and an index to point at one of it's sons.

Returned value(s): None.
Called by: Translater, Rearrange passive construction.
Calling: Pop lex information (recursively).
The subroutine processes the tree structure to bring semantic information to the tops.

No. 29
Function Name: Read Sent.
Arguments: None.
Returned value(s): A string in the form of a labeled bracketing.
Called by: Translater.
Note: The subroutine reads a sentence from an input dataset.

No. 30
Function Name: Rearrange passive construction.
Arguments: A pointer to the case candidate with the form of a PP with preposition *door* (by), a pointer to it's father and an index to point at the NP with subject function.
Returned value(s): None.
Called by: Interpret sentence.
Note: The subroutine performs depassivization transformations.

No. 31
Function Name: Redundancies.
Arguments: None.
Returned value(s): None.
Called by: Translater.
Note: The subroutine adds redundant features to lexical items.

No. 32
Function Name: Retrieve L I.
Arguments: A pointer to a node of the tree structure.
Returned value(s): None.
Called by: Consult lexicon.
Note: The subroutine links a certain terminal symbol node with an element of the lexicon.

No. 33
Function Name: Set verb features.
Arguments: A pointer to a main verb.
Returned value(s): None.
Called by: Verb features.
Note: The subroutine administrates the auxiliaries.

No. 34
Function Name: Test claims.
Arguments: A pointer to a caseframe of the main verb considered, a pointer to the case candidate considered, information about passive or active voice, the case function concerned.
Returned value(s): True or False.
Called by: All case claims met.
Note: The subroutine tests whether a constituent is marked for certain properties.

No. 35
Function Name: Test sequences.
Arguments: An index to refer to a main verb.
Returned value(s): An integer to indicate the number of different sequences to be tested.
Called by: Interpret sentence.

No. 36
Function Name: Translater.
Arguments: None.
Returned value(s): None.
Called by: Main program.
Calling: Load lexicon, Redundancies, Read sentence, Consult lexicon, Pop lex information, Set main features, Detopicalize resetverb, Find nodes(VERB), Administrate satellites, Interpret sentence.

No. 37
Function Name: WH comp.
Arguments: A pointer to a node of the tree structure.
Returned value(s): If true, a pointer to that node.
Called by: different functions.
Note: The function returns True (and so a pointer to a node) if the node ind has +WH features.

No. 38
Function Name: WH compontop.
Arguments: A pointer to a main verb of the sentence.
Returned value(s): if found, a pointer to a certain node.
Called by: Administrate satellites.
Calling: Bridge verb.
Note: the function which is called iteratively for different verbs retrieves a WH-constituent that may have been detected in an earlier instance in connection with the verb on top of a

socalled bridge, reaching from this verb (the argument) as far as possible upward, but every time it is called only to the next higher verb.

No. 39
Function Name: Write result.
Arguments: A pointer to a certain node.
Returned value(s): A labeled bracketing.
Called by: Different places.
Note: The function is used as the main output routine. It may be parameterized for giving simple or more detailed information about the tree.

# 3 TEST OF CASE CANDIDATES

In order to fully account for the way decisions are made by CASUS about the semantic role to be played by a certain case candidate I give all details of the subroutine 'Acceptable cand for case'. The description will be merely enumerative and will lack all discussion.

1 If not 'All case claims met', continue with Second Test; else go to the statements, regarding the case function concerned.

2 Agentive. If the case candidate is a PC, fail. If the sentence's voice is active, continue with Agentive Active. If the sentence's voice is passive: if the case candidate is the inserted dummy, succeed. If not: if the case candidate has the feature accusative, succeed, else fail.
Agentive Active: if the case candidate does not agree with the finite verb, fail. If the case candidate has the nominative form, succeed, else fail.

3 Dative. If the case candidate is not both accusative and nominative, continue with Dative second. If a constituent has been assigned to the case agentive, succeed. If the case candidate agrees with the verb concerned, succeed, else fail.
Dative second. If the case candidate has the form of accusative, continue with Dative third. Else, if a constituent has been assigned to the case agentive, fail. If the case candidate agrees with the verb concerned, succeed, else fail.
Dative third. If the case candidate has the form of a PC: if it starts with the preposition *aan* or *voor*, succeed, else fail. If it is not a PC: if a constituent has been assigned to the case agentive, succeed, else fail.

4 Objective. If the case candidate is not a PC, NC, CC, W1 or W2, fail. Else, continue with the tests for Factitive.

5 Factitive. If the sentence's voice is active, continue with Factitive Active. If the case candidate does not agree with the finite verb, fail. Else, continue.
Factitive Active. If the case candidate is not accusative succeed. If the case concerned is Objective, succeed. If the case candidate has the features 'time' or 'place', fail; else, succeed.

6 Instrumental. If the case candidate is an NC and the case Agentive or Dative has been assigned to some constituent, fail. Else, succeed.

7 Locative. If the case candidate is a W1, CC or a pronoun, fail. If the case candidate has the lexical feature 'locative', succeed. Else, fail.

8 Attribute. Succeed.

9 Second Test. If the case function concerned is not Instrumental, fail. Else, if the case functions Agentive or Dative have been assigned, fail. Else, if the case candidate is not an NC, fail. Else, if the case candidate has the lexical feature 'concrete' succeed; else, fail.

# 4 AN EXAMPLE ANALYSIS

In this section a trace is shown of the analysis of a sentence by CASUS. The trace has been produced by the program and has not been postedited. Only labeled bracketings have been changed into treediagrams afterwards.

The different tries at the level of the different verbs of the sentence should be regarded in connection with the lexical definitions. Therefore the relevant part of the lexicon is shown:

```
WIE$NK$PRON$2,1,,1,2,2,*$$@
DENK$WW$SS$
  DAT(),OBJ(+ABS),*
  DAT(),OBJ(+CCR/PC/AAN),*
  $DENK,DENKT,DENKE,DENKEND,GEDACHT,DACHT,DACHTEN, $@
JE$NK$PRON$1,1,0,1,1,2,*$$@
DAT$VW$GR$+ABS*$$@
JAN$NK$SU$1,,,,0,1,1,1,0,1,*$,$@
VERTEL$WW$--$
  AGE(),DAT(?),OBJ(+ABS),*
  $VERTELT,VERTELT,VERTELLE,VERTELLEND,VERTELD, VERTELDE,VERTEL-
DEN,$@
MUZIEK$NK$SU$0,,,0,0,1,,0,0,1,*$$@
VAAK$BW$$+TEMP*$$@
LELIJK$AK$$$$@
VIND$WW$--$
  DAT(),ATT(+NON/AJ/),*
  AGE(),OBJ(),*
  $VINDT,VINDT,VINDE,VINDEND,GEVONDEN,VOND,VONDEN$@
```

On the right side of the pages showing the trace, some comments are added for a better understanding. It is indicated which case frame of the verb is going to be tested, whether it is tested with or without using the WH-constituent and which hypothesis about the sequence of the candidates will be considered. The trace contains mainly information about the case function that is tested (by the function 'Acceptable cand for case') in relation with a certain case candidate. Concerning both the function and the candidate, information is displayed of the following contents: 1. the case function (three characters), 2. the lexical form of the verb concerned, 3. the lexical word which characterizes the candidate, 4. the syntactic category of the candidate, 5. the features of the candidate for this function, as claimed by the verb, 6. the actual semantic features of the candidate to be tested, displayed after the marking *FEATURES*. The claimed features of the candidate are often enumerated as a set of alternatives.

The tracing:

1 WIE DENK JE DAT JAN VERTELDE DAT MUZIEK V

AAK LELIJK VOND.

After Detopicalization and Resetting of V:

(1)

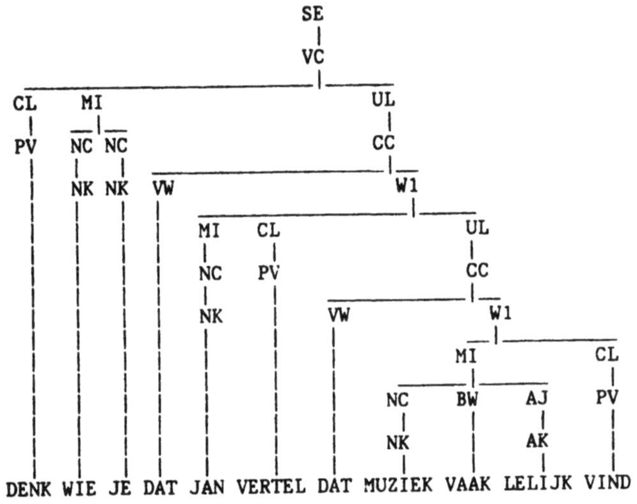


Verb No. 1 DENK

1 : DENK — First frame, +WH,

Change sequence cases 3 — first sequence.

1 Case Candidates * (NC(NK-JE))

2 Case Candidates * (CC(VW-DAT)(W1-(MI-(N
C-(NK-JAN)))(CL-(PV-VERTEL))(UL-(CC-(VW-DAT)
(W1-(MI-(NC-(NK-MUZIEK))(BW-VAAK)(AJ-(AK-LEL
IJK)))(CL-(PV-VIND)))))))

3 Case Candidates * (NC(NK-WIE))

Acceptable DAT DENK : JE - NC +ANI F
EATURES: 1,1,1,1,,,,1,,1,1,1,0,1,1,2,*

Allocated DAT

Acceptable OBJ DENK : DAT - CC +ABS+ACC
/NC +ABS+ACC/CC/DAT +ABS+ACC/CC/OF +ABS+ACC/
W2 FEATURES: +ABS+ACC+NOM+PE3+ABS*

Allocated OBJ

Acceptable LOK DENK : WIE - NC ? +LOK
FEATURES: 1,1,1,1,,,,1,,1,2,1,,1,2,2,*

Analysis fails.

Change sequence cases 2 — Second sequence.

1 Case Candidates * (NC(NK-JE))

2 Case Candidates * (NC(NK-WIE))

3 Case Candidates * (CC(VW-DAT)(W1-(MI-(N

C-(NK-JAN)))(CL-(PV-VERTEL))(UL-(CC-(VW-DAT)
(W1-(MI-(NC-(NK-MUZIEK))(BW-VAAK)(AJ-(AK-LEL
IJK)))(CL-(PV-VIND)))))))
Acceptable DAT DENK : JE - NC +ANI F
EATURES: 1,1,1,1,,,,1,,1,1,1,0,1,1,2,*
Allocated DAT
Acceptable OBJ DENK : WIE - NC +ABS+ACC
/NC +ABS+ACC/CC/DAT +ABS+ACC/CC/OF +ABS+ACC/
W2 FEATURES: 1,1,1,1,,,,1,,1,2,1,,1,2,2,*
Analysis fails.

Change sequence cases 1 — Third sequence.
1 Case Candidates * (NC(NK-WIE))
2 Case Candidates * (NC(NK-JE))
3 Case Candidates * (CC(VW-DAT)(W1-(MI-(N
C-(NK-JAN)))(CL-(PV-VERTEL))(UL-(CC-(VW-DAT)
(W1-(MI-(NC-(NK-MUZIEK))(BW-VAAK)(AJ-(AK-LEL
IJK)))(CL-(PV-VIND)))))))
Acceptable DAT DENK : WIE - NC +ANI
FEATURES: 1,1,1,1,,,,1,,1,2,1,,1,2,2,*
Analysis fails.

2 : DENK — Second frame, +WH, first sequence.

Change sequence cases 3
1 Case Candidates * (NC(NK-JE))
2 Case Candidates * (CC(VW-DAT)(W1-(MI-(N
C-(NK-JAN)))(CL-(PV-VERTEL))(UL-(CC-(VW-DAT)
(W1-(MI-(NC-(NK-MUZIEK))(BW-VAAK)(AJ-(AK-LEL
IJK)))(CL-(PV-VIND)))))))
3 Case Candidates * (NC(NK-WIE))
Acceptable DAT DENK : JE - NC +ANI F
EATURES: 1,1,1,1,,,,1,,1,1,1,0,1,1,2,*
Allocated DAT
Acceptable OBJ DENK : DAT - CC +CCR/PC/
AAN FEATURES: +ABS+ACC+NOM+PE3+ABS*
Analysis fails.

Change sequence cases 2 — Second sequence.
1 Case Candidates * (NC(NK-JE))
2 Case Candidates * (NC(NK-WIE))
3 Case Candidates * (CC(VW-DAT)(W1-(MI-(N
C-(NK-JAN)))(CL-(PV-VERTEL))(UL-(CC-(VW-DAT)
(W1-(MI-(NC-(NK-MUZIEK))(BW-VAAK)(AJ-(AK-LEL
IJK)))(CL-(PV-VIND)))))))
Acceptable DAT DENK : JE - NC +ANI F
EATURES: 1,1,1,1,,,,1,,1,1,1,0,1,1,2,*

Allocated DAT
Acceptable OBJ DENK : WIE - NC +CCR/PC/
AAN FEATURES: 1,1,1,1,,,,1,,1,2,1,,1,2,2,
*
Analysis fails.

Change sequence cases 1 — Third sequence.
1 Case Candidates * (NC(NK-WIE))
2 Case Candidates * (NC(NK-JE))
3 Case Candidates * (CC(VW-DAT)(W1-(MI-(N
C-(NK-JAN)))(CL-(PV-VERTEL))(UL-(CC-(VW-DAT)
(W1-(MI-(NC-(NK-MUZIEK))(BW-VAAK)(AJ-(AK-LEL
IJK)))(CL-(PV-VIND)))))))
Acceptable DAT DENK : WIE - NC +ANI
FEATURES: 1,1,1,1,,,,1,,1,2,1,,1,2,2,*
Analysis fails.

3 : DENK — First frame, -WH,
Change sequence cases 2 — first sequence.
1 Case Candidates * (CC(VW-DAT)(W1-(MI-(N
C-(NK-JAN)))(CL-(PV-VERTEL))(UL-(CC-(VW-DAT)
(W1-(MI-(NC-(NK-MUZIEK))(BW-VAAK)(AJ-(AK-LEL
IJK)))(CL-(PV-VIND)))))))
2 Case Candidates * (NC(NK-JE))
Acceptable DAT DENK : DAT - CC +ANI
FEATURES: +ABS+ACC+NOM+PE3+ABS*
Analysis fails.

Change sequence cases 1 — Second sequence.
1 Case Candidates * (NC(NK-JE))
2 Case Candidates * (CC(VW-DAT)(W1-(MI-(N
C-(NK-JAN)))(CL-(PV-VERTEL))(UL-(CC-(VW-DAT)
(W1-(MI-(NC-(NK-MUZIEK))(BW-VAAK)(AJ-(AK-LEL
IJK)))(CL-(PV-VIND)))))))
Acceptable DAT DENK : JE - NC +ANI F
EATURES: 1,1,1,1,,,,1,,1,1,1,0,1,1,2,*
Allocated DAT
Acceptable OBJ DENK : DAT - CC +ABS+ACC
/NC +ABS+ACC/CC/DAT +ABS+ACC/CC/OF +ABS+ACC/
W2 FEATURES: +ABS+ACC+NOM+PE3+ABS*
Allocated OBJ
> DENK Analysis succeeds:

(2)

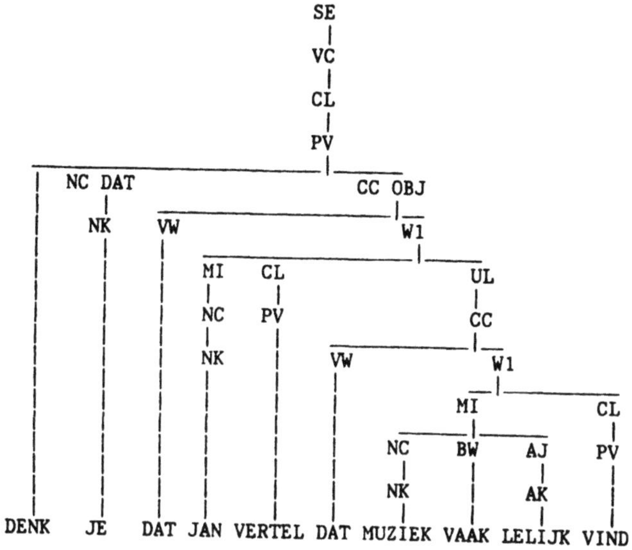


Verb No. 2 VERTELDE
1 : VERTELDE

First frame, +WH, first sequence.

Change sequence cases 3
1 Case Candidates * (NC(NK-JAN))
2 Case Candidates * (CC(VW-DAT)(W1-(MI-(N
C-(NK-MUZIEK))(BW-VAAK)(AJ-(AK-LELIJK)))(CL
(PV-VIND))))
3 Case Candidates * (NC(NK-WIE))
  Acceptable AGE VERTELDE : JAN - NC +ANI
/NC  FEATURES: 1,1,1,1,0,1,1,1,0,1,*+ACC+D
AT+NOM+PE3+SIN
Allocated AGE
  Acceptable DAT VERTELDE : DAT - CC ? +AN
I  FEATURES: +ABS+ACC+NOM+PE3+ABS*
  Acceptable OBJ VERTELDE : DAT - CC +ABS
+ACC/NC +ABS+ACC/CC/DAT +ABS+ACC/CC/OF +ABS+
ACC/W2 FEATURES: +ABS+ACC+NOM+PE3+ABS*
Allocated OBJ
  Acceptable LOK VERTELDE : WIE - NC ? +LO
K  FEATURES: 1,1,1,1,,,,1,,1,2,1,,1,2,2,*
Analysis fails.

Change sequence cases 2

Second sequence.

1 Case Candidates * (NC(NK-JAN))
2 Case Candidates * (NC(NK-WIE))
3 Case Candidates * (CC(VW-DAT)(W1-(MI-(N

C-(NK-MUZIEK))(BW-VAAK)(AJ-(AK-LELIJK)))(CL
(PV-VIND))))
  Acceptable AGE VERTELDE : JAN - NC +ANI
/NC  FEATURES: 1,1,1,1,0,1,1,1,0,1,*+ACC+D
AT+NOM+PE3+SIN+SIN+PE3
Allocated AGE
  Acceptable DAT VERTELDE : WIE - NC ? +AN
I  FEATURES: 1,1,1,1,,,,1,,1,2,1,,1,2,2,*
Allocated DAT

  Acceptable OBJ VERTELDE : DAT - CC +ABS
+ACC/NC +ABS+ACC/CC/DAT +ABS+ACC/CC/OF +ABS+
ACC/W2 FEATURES: +ABS+ACC+NOM+PE3+ABS*
Allocated OBJ
> VERTELDE Analysis succeeds:

(3)

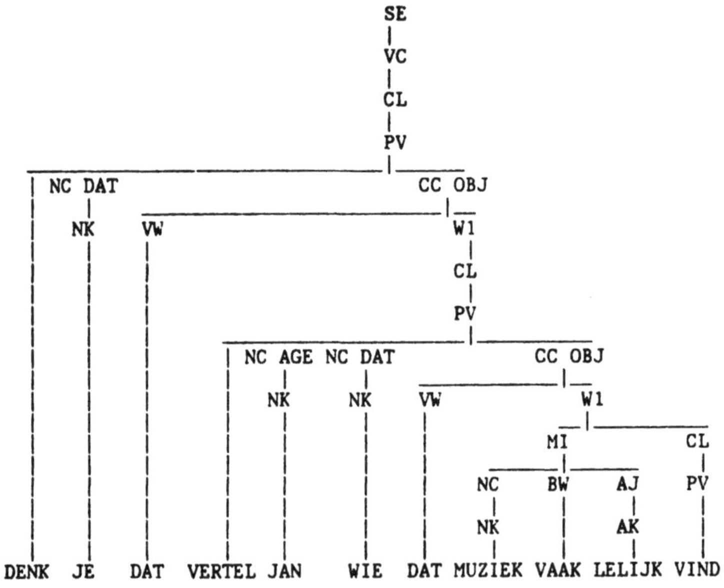


Verb No. 3 VOND
1 : VOND    First frame, +WH.
2 : VOND    Second frame, +WH.

3 : VOND    First frame, -WH.
Change sequence cases 1
1 Case Candidates * (NC(NK-MUZIEK))
2 Case Candidates * (BW-VAAK)
3 Case Candidates * (AJ(AK-LELIJK))
  Acceptable DAT VOND : MUZIEK - NC +ANI

FEATURES: 0,,,0,0,1,,0,0,1,*+ACC+DAT+NOM+
PE3+SIN
Analysis fails.

4 : VOND — Second frame, -WH.
Change sequence cases 1
1 Case Candidates * (NC(NK-MUZIEK))
2 Case Candidates * (BW-VAAK)
3 Case Candidates * (AJ(AK-LELIJK))
Acceptable AGE VOND : MUZIEK - NC +ANI/
NC FEATURES: 0,,,0,0,1,,0,0,1,*+ACC+DAT+N
OM+PE3+SIN
Analysis fails.

Verb No. 2 VERTELDE
1 : VERTELDE — First frame, +WH, third sequence.
Change sequence cases 1
1 Case Candidates * (NC(NK-WIE))
2 Case Candidates * (NC(NK-JAN))
3 Case Candidates * (CC(VW-DAT)(W1-(MI-(N
C-(NK-MUZIEK))(BW-VAAK)(AJ-(AK-LELIJK)))(CL
(PV-VIND))))
Acceptable AGE VERTELDE : WIE - NC +ANI
/NC FEATURES: 1,1,1,1,,,,1,,1,2,1,,1,2,2,
*
Allocated AGE
Acceptable DAT VERTELDE : JAN - NC ? +AN
I FEATURES: 1,1,1,1,0,1,1,1,0,1,*+ACC+DAT
+NOM+PE3+SIN+SIN+PE3+SIN+PE3
Allocated DAT
Acceptable OBJ VERTELDE : DAT - CC +ABS
+ACC/NC +ABS+ACC/CC/DAT +ABS+ACC/CC/OF +ABS+
ACC/W2 FEATURES: +ABS+ACC+NOM+PE3+ABS*
Allocated OBJ
> VERTELDE Analysis succeeds: — See tree (4) on next page.

Verb No. 3 VOND
1 : VOND — First frame, +WH.
2 : VOND — Second frame, +WH.

3 : VOND — First frame, -WH.
Change sequence cases 1
1 Case Candidates * (NC(NK-MUZIEK))
2 Case Candidates * (BW-VAAK)
3 Case Candidates * (AJ(AK-LELIJK))
Acceptable DAT VOND : MUZIEK - NC +ANI
FEATURES: 0,,,0,0,1,,0,0,1,*+ACC+DAT+NOM+
PE3+SIN
Analysis fails.

(4)

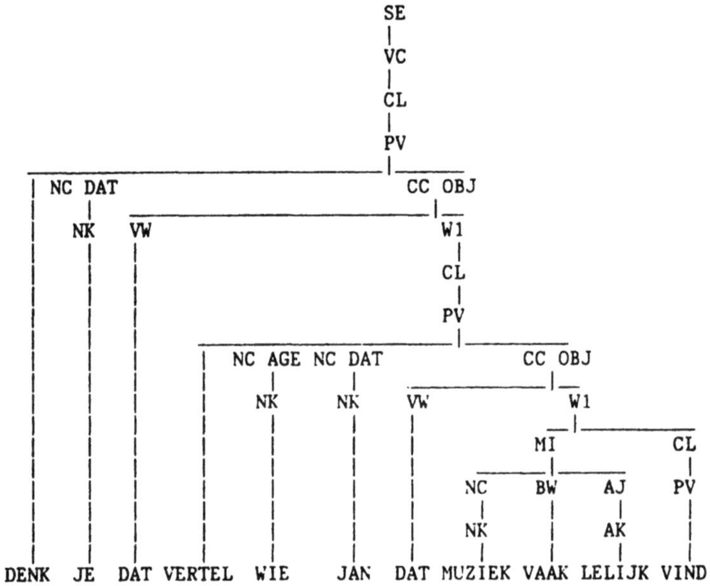


4 : VOND — Second frame, -WH.

Change sequence cases 1

1 Case Candidates * (NC(NK-MUZIEK))

2 Case Candidates * (BW-VAAK)

3 Case Candidates * (AJ(AK-LELIJK))

Acceptable AGE VOND : MUZIEK - NC +ANI/
NC FEATURES: 0,,,0,0,1,,0,0,1,*+ACC+DAT+N
OM+PE3+SIN

Analysis fails.

Verb No. 2 VERTELDE

2 : VERTELDE — First frame, -WH.

Change sequence cases 1

1 Case Candidates * (NC(NK-JAN))

2 Case Candidates * (CC(VW-DAT)(W1-(MI-(N
C-(NK-MUZIEK))(BW-VAAK)(AJ-(AK-LELIJK)))(CL
(PV-VIND))))

Acceptable AGE VERTELDE : JAN - NC +ANI
/NC FEATURES: 1,1,1,1,0,1,1,1,0,1,*+ACC+D
AT+NOM+PE3+SIN+SIN+PE3+SIN+PE3

Allocated AGE

Acceptable DAT VERTELDE : DAT - CC ? +AN
I FEATURES: +ABS+ACC+NOM+PE3+ABS*
Acceptable OBJ VERTELDE : DAT - CC +ABS
+ACC/NC +ABS+ACC/CC/DAT +ABS+ACC/CC/OF +ABS+
ACC/W2 FEATURES: +ABS+ACC+NOM+PE3+ABS*
Allocated OBJ
> VERTELDE Analysis succeeds:

(5)

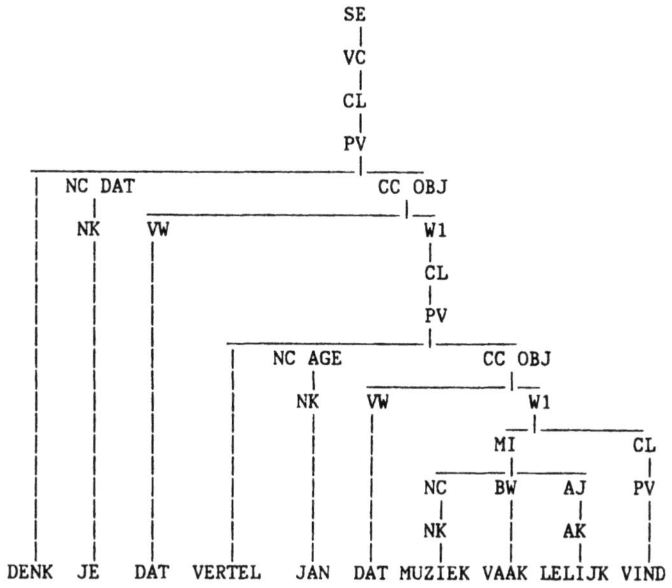


Verb No. 3 VOND
1 : VOND — First frame, +WH,
Change sequence cases 4 — first sequence.
1 Case Candidates * (NC(NK-MUZIEK))
2 Case Candidates * (BW-VAAK)
3 Case Candidates * (AJ(AK-LELIJK))
4 Case Candidates * (NC(NK-WIE))
Acceptable DAT VOND : MUZIEK - NC +ANI
FEATURES: 0,,,0,0,1,,0,0,1,*+ACC+DAT+NOM+
PE3+SIN
Analysis fails.

Change sequence cases 3 — Second sequence.
1 Case Candidates * (NC(NK-MUZIEK))
2 Case Candidates * (BW-VAAK)
3 Case Candidates * (NC(NK-WIE))
4 Case Candidates * (AJ(AK-LELIJK))
Acceptable DAT VOND : MUZIEK - NC +ANI
FEATURES: 0,,,0,0,1,,0,0,1,*+ACC+DAT+NOM+
PE3+SIN
Analysis fails.

Change sequence cases 2 — Third sequence.
1 Case Candidates * (NC(NK-MUZIEK))
2 Case Candidates * (NC(NK-WIE))
3 Case Candidates * (BW-VAAK)
4 Case Candidates * (AJ(AK-LELIJK))
Acceptable DAT VOND : MUZIEK - NC +ANI
FEATURES: 0,,,0,0,1,,0,0,1,*+ACC+DAT+NOM+
PE3+SIN
Analysis fails.

Change sequence cases 1 — Fourth sequence. (See note 29.)
1 Case Candidates * (NC(NK-WIE))
2 Case Candidates * (NC(NK-MUZIEK))
3 Case Candidates * (BW-VAAK)
4 Case Candidates * (AJ(AK-LELIJK))
Acceptable DAT VOND : WIE - NC +ANI
FEATURES: 1,1,1,1,,,,1,,1,2,1,,1,2,2,*+SIN+P
E3
Allocated DAT
Acceptable OBJ VOND : MUZIEK - NC +NON
FEATURES: 0,,,0,0,1,,0,0,1,*+ACC+DAT+NOM+
PE3+SIN
Allocated OBJ
Acceptable ATT VOND : VAAK - BW +NON/AJ
/ FEATURES: +TEMP*
Acceptable ATT VOND : LELIJK - AJ +NON/
AJ/ FEATURES:
Allocated ATT
Allocated OPER
> VOND Analysis succeeds: — See tree (6) on next page.

2 : VOND — Second frame, +WH,

Change sequence cases 4 — first sequence.
1 Case Candidates * (NC(NK-MUZIEK))
2 Case Candidates * (BW-VAAK)
3 Case Candidates * (AJ(AK-LELIJK))
4 Case Candidates * (NC(NK-WIE))
Acceptable AGE VOND : MUZIEK - NC +ANI/
NC FEATURES: 0,,,0,0,1,,0,0,1,*+ACC+DAT+N
OM+PE3+SIN
Analysis fails.

(6)

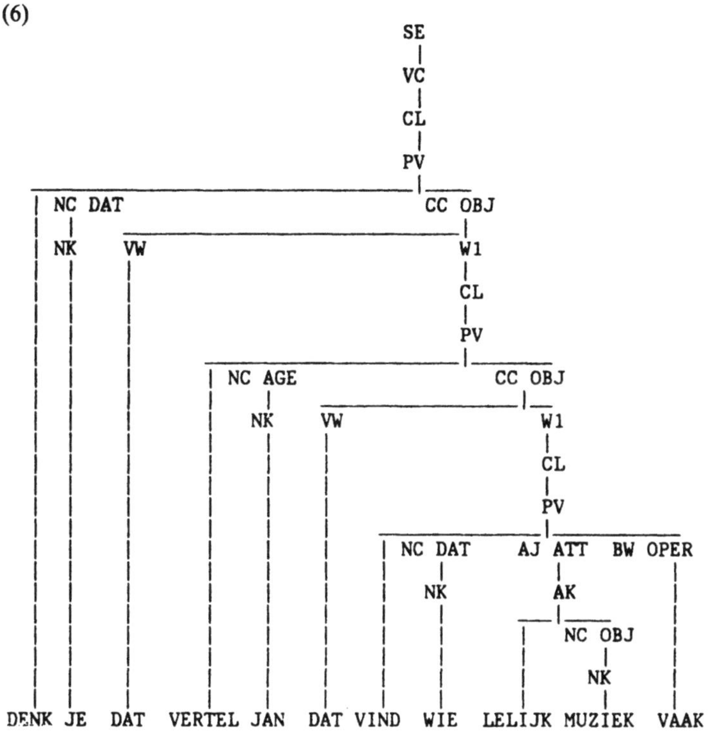


Change sequence cases 3 — Second sequence.
1 Case Candidates * (NC(NK-MUZIEK))
2 Case Candidates * (BW-VAAK)
3 Case Candidates * (NC(NK-WIE))
4 Case Candidates * (AJ(AK-LELIJK))
Acceptable AGE VOND : MUZIEK - NC +ANI/
NC FEATURES: 0,,,0,0,1,,0,0,1,*+ACC+DAT+N
OM+PE3+SIN
Analysis fails.

Change sequence cases 2 — Third sequence.
1 Case Candidates * (NC(NK-MUZIEK))
2 Case Candidates * (NC(NK-WIE))
3 Case Candidates * (BW-VAAK)
4 Case Candidates * (AJ(AK-LELIJK))
Acceptable AGE VOND : MUZIEK - NC +ANI/
NC FEATURES: 0,,,0,0,1,,0,0,1,*+ACC+DAT+N
OM+PE3+SIN
Analysis fails.

Change sequence cases 1 — Fourth sequence.
1 Case Candidates * (NC(NK-WIE)) — (See note 29.)

2 Case Candidates * (NC(NK-MUZIEK))
3 Case Candidates * (BW-VAAK)
4 Case Candidates * (AJ(AK-LELIJK))
  Acceptable AGE VOND : WIE - NC +ANI/NC
 FEATURES: 1,1,1,1,,,,1,,1,2,1,,1,2,2,*+SI
N+PE3
Allocated AGE
  Acceptable OBJ VOND : MUZIEK - NC +NON/
NC FEATURES: 0,,,0,0,1,,0,0,1,*+ACC+DAT+N
OM+PE3+SIN
Allocated OBJ
  Acceptable LOK VOND : VAAK - BW ? +LOK
 FEATURES: +TEMP*
Allocated OPER
> VOND Analysis succeeds:

(7)

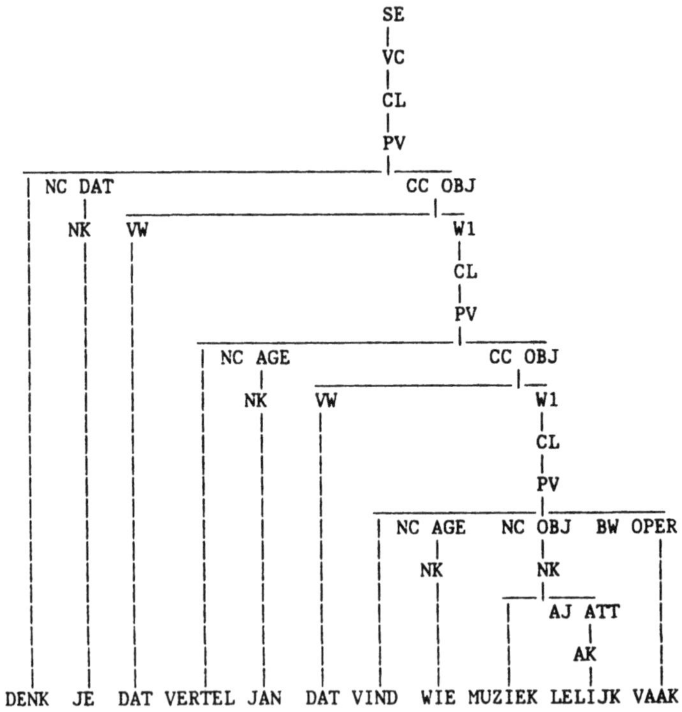


3 : VOND First frame, -WH.
Change sequence cases 1
1 Case Candidates * (NC(NK-MUZIEK))
2 Case Candidates * (BW-VAAK)
3 Case Candidates * (AJ(AK-LELIJK))
  Acceptable DAT VOND : MUZIEK - NC +ANI
 FEATURES: 0,,,0,0,1,,0,0,1,*+ACC+DAT+NOM+
PE3+SIN
Analysis fails.

4 : VOND

Second frame, -WH.

Change sequence cases 1
1 Case Candidates * (NC(NK-MUZIEK))
2 Case Candidates * (BW-VAAK)
3 Case Candidates * (AJ(AK-LELIJK))
Acceptable AGE VOND : MUZIEK - NC +ANI/
NC FEATURES: 0,,,0,0,1,,0,0,1,*+ACC+DAT+N
OM+PE3+SIN
Analysis fails.

Verb No. 2 VERTELDE
3 : VERTELDE

No alternatives left.

Analysis fails.

Verb No. 1 DENK
4 : DENK

Second frame, -WH, first sequence.

Change sequence cases 2
1 Case Candidates * (CC(VW-DAT)(W1-(CL-(P
V-VERTEL(NC AGE-(NK-JAN))(CC OBJ-(VW-DAT)(W1
-(CL-(PV-VIND))))))))
2 Case Candidates * (NC(NK-JE))
Acceptable DAT DENK : DAT - CC +ANI
FEATURES: +ABS+ACC+NOM+PE3+ABS*
Analysis fails.

Second sequence.

Change sequence cases 1
1 Case Candidates * (NC(NK-JE))
2 Case Candidates * (CC(VW-DAT)(W1-(CL-(P
V-VERTEL(NC AGE-(NK-JAN))(CC OBJ-(VW-DAT)(W1
-(CL-(PV-VIND))))))))
Acceptable DAT DENK : JE - NC +ANI F
EATURES: 1,1,1,1,,,,1,,1,1,1,0,1,1,2,*
Allocated DAT
Acceptable OBJ DENK : DAT - CC +CCR/PC/
AAN FEATURES: +ABS+ACC+NOM+PE3+ABS*
Analysis fails.

The sentence receives two different SELANCA-representations, the one with the reading of *often thinking that music is ugly* and the other with that of *finding often music in an ugly state*.

Finally, the normal output dataset of CASUS is shown. It should be noticed, that also this representation is not a full account of the information that is present for CASUS. For other purposes (experiments in automatic translation), the structure is output with detailed semantic feature specifications.

INVOER AMAZON *** 1 WIE DENK JE DAT JAN VERTELDE DAT MUZIEK
VAAK LELIJK VOND.

OUTPUT AMAZON *** 1 (SE (NC (NK WIE))(VC (PV DENK)(MI (NC (NK J E)))(UL (CC (VW DAT)(W1 (MI (NC (NK JAN)))(CL (PV VERTELDE))(UL (CC (VW DAT)(W1 (MI (NC (NK MUZIEK))(BW-VAAK)(AJ (AK LELIJK)))(C L (PV VOND))))))))))#AMAZON 83-1E ANALYSE##

OUTPUT CASUS84 *** 1 (SE-(VC-(CL-(PV-DENK(NC DAT-(NK-JE))(CC O BJ-(VW-DAT)(W1-(CL-(PV-VERTEL(NC AGE-(NK-JAN))(CC OBJ-(VW-DAT)(W 1-(CL-(PV-VIND(NC DAT-(NK-WIE))(AJ ATT-(AK-LELIJK(NC OBJ-(NK MUZ IEK))))(BW OPER-VAAK))))))))))))#01/24/84-710 MS##

OUTPUT CASUS84 *** 1 (SE-(VC-(CL-(PV-DENK(NC DAT-(NK-JE))(CC O BJ-(VW-DAT)(W1-(CL-(PV-VERTEL(NC AGE-(NK-JAN))(CC OBJ-(VW-DAT)(W 1-(CL-(PV-VIND(NC AGE-(NK-WIE))(NC OBJ-(NK-MUZIEK(AJ ATT-(AK LEL IJK))))(BW OPER-VAAK))))))))))))#01/24/84-760 MS##

The second analysis of the sentence by AMAZON is not considered here. It is not interesting since it considered the adjective *lelijk* to be an adverb.

# 5 A SAMPLE TRACING OF AMAZON(80)

This tracing shows the interaction between the user and the analyzer AMAZON(80). It has been obtained from a kind of log-book which is updated continuously by AMAZON while executing. Note that AMAZON(80) performs also a syntactic analysis. It is shown in labeled bracketings. Some brief commentary is added in lower case characters.

| | |
|---|---|
| * * * * * ZITTING AMAZON (80) * * * * * | |
| HET IS VANDAAG 03/14/84 | |
| ATTENTIE - HET DIEPTEBEREIK IS : 8 | |
| DEBUG KLAAR OP VERZOEK. | |
| ** ADS(PATRICK) | Adding a noun. |
| -PATRICK- TOEGEVOEGD AAN DE GRAMMATICA | Answer of the system. |
| ** ADS(LUCIE) | |
| -LUCIE- TOEGEVOEGD AAN DE GRAMMATICA | |
| ** ADS(BACH) | |
| -BACH- TOEGEVOEGD AAN DE GRAMMATICA | |
| ** ADW(ZING) | Adding a verb. |
| -ZING- TOEGEVOEGD AAN DE GRAMMATICA | |
| ** GRA | Syntactic analysis |
| GRAMMATICALE ANALYSE | option chosen. |
| *** SENT/PATRICK HOORT ZINGEN | String offered. |
| ALLES BEKEND - ENTER OF DEBUG | Words are known. |
| | |
| WAT KIEST U VOOR HOORT (HVIP VSUBP ) ? | Choice to user. |
| (GEKOZEN HVIP) | Choice made by user. |
| ANALYSE; START DOOR MET ENTER OF "DEBUG" | |
| ** MET SUCCES ONTLEED ** | Analysis succeeds. |
| (*SE*(*NC*(*NK*PATRICK *NK*)*NC*)(*VC*(*13*HOORT *13*)(*CL*(*VI* ZINGEN *VI*)*CL*)*VC*)*SE*)-177MS | Milliseconds used. |
| | |
| TYP "JA" VOOR ANALYSE VAN HET RESULTAAT | |
| *** SENT/PATRICK HOORT LUCIE ZINGEN | Second string. |
| ALLES BEKEND - ENTER OF DEBUG | |
| WAT KIEST U VOOR HOORT (HVIP VSUBP ) ? | |
| (GEKOZEN HVIP) | |
| ANALYSE; START DOOR MET ENTER OF "DEBUG" | |
| ** MET SUCCES ONTLEED ** | |
| (*SE*(*NC*(*NK*PATRICK *NK*)*NC*)(*VC*(*13*HOORT *13*)(*MI*(*NC* (*NK*LUCIE *NK*)*NC*)*MI*)(*CL*(*VI*ZINGEN *VI*)*CL*)*VC*)*SE*) 210MS | |

```
TYP "JA" VOOR ANALYSE VAN HET RESULTAAT
*** SENT/PATRICK HOORT LUCIE BACH ZINGEN
ALLES BEKEND - ENTER OF DEBUG
WAT KIEST U VOOR HOORT (HVIP VSUBP ) ?
 (GEKOZEN HVIP)
ANALYSE; START DOOR MET ENTER OF "DEBUG"
** MET SUCCES ONTLEED **
(*SE*(*NC*(*NK*PATRICK *NK*)*NC*)(*VC*(*13*HOORT *13*)(*MI*(*NC*
(*NK*LUCIE *NK*)*NC*)(*NC*(*NK*BACH *NK*)*NC*)*MI*)(*CL*(*VI*ZIN
GEN *VI*)*CL*)*VC*)*SE*)-250MS
TYP "JA" VOOR ANALYSE VAN HET RESULTAAT
*** SENT/PATRICK SCHIJNT LUCIE TE HOREN ZINGEN
ALLES BEKEND - ENTER OF DEBUG
WAT KIEST U VOOR SCHIJNT (HVTIP VSUBP ) ?
 (GEKOZEN HVTIP)
WAT KIEST U VOOR TE HOREN (HVITI VSUBTI ) ?
 (GEKOZEN HVITI)
ANALYSE; START DOOR MET ENTER OF "DEBUG"
** MET SUCCES ONTLEED **
(*SE*(*NC*(*NK*PATRICK *NK*)*NC*)(*VC*(*12*SCHIJNT *12*)(*MI*(*N
C*(*NK*LUCIE *NK*)*NC*)*MI*)(*CL*(*23*TE HOREN *23*)(*VI*ZINGEN
*VI*)*CL*)*VC*)*SE*)-300MS
TYP "JA" VOOR ANALYSE VAN HET RESULTAAT
*** SENT/PATERICK PROBEERT LUCIE TE HOREN ZINGEN
WOORD PATERICK IS NIET BEKEND.
 DEBUG - ANALYSE VAN GROEP ONMOGELIJK
*** SENT/PATRICK PROBEERT LUCIE TE HOREN ZINGEN
ALLES BEKEND - ENTER OF DEBUG
WAT KIEST U VOOR PROBEERT (HVTIP VSUBP ) ?
 (GEKOZEN HVTIP)
WAT KIEST U VOOR TE HOREN (HVITI VSUBTI ) ?
 (GEKOZEN HVITI)
ANALYSE; START DOOR MET ENTER OF "DEBUG"
** MET SUCCES ONTLEED **
(*SE*(*NC*(*NK*PATRICK *NK*)*NC*)(*VC*(*12*PROBEERT *12*)(*MI*(*
NC*(*NK*LUCIE *NK*)*NC*)*MI*)(*CL*(*23*TE HOREN *23*)(*VI*ZINGEN
 *VI*)*CL*)*VC*)*SE*)-220MS
TYP "JA" VOOR ANALYSE VAN HET RESULTAAT
*EINDE DEBUG*
HOE VERDER? - ANTWOORD "RETURN", "START" OF "END" End option chosen.
EINDE ZITTING AMAZON ; EXECUTIE-TIJD WAS 1713 MILLISEC.
HET AANTAL AANGEBODEN GROEPEN WAS 5
```

Bei Fragen zur Produktsicherheit wenden Sie sich bitte an:
If you have any questions regarding product safety,
please contact:

Walter de Gruyter GmbH
Genthiner Straße 13
10785 Berlin
productsafety@degruyterbrill.com